GIRL DIRECTOR

A HOW-TO GUIDE FOR THE FIRST-TIME FLAT-BROKE FILM MAKER (AND VIDEO MAKER)

Written by
Andrea Richards
Foreword by **Allison Anders**
Designed by Amy Inouye
Illustrations by Elizabeth McCalli

ISBN: 1-931497-00-1
Library of Congress Catalog-in-Publication Number: 2001086654

Printed in Hong Kong

GIRL PRESS

slightly dangerous books for girl mavericks
www.girlpress.com

a division of 17th Street Productions, an Alloy Online company

GIRL PRESS books are available for retail distribution through:

LPC Group
1436 West Randolph Street
Chicago, IL 60607
(800) 626-4330
www.coolbooks.com

GIRL PRESS books are available at special quantity discounts to use as premiums, sales promotions, or for use in education programs. For more information, please write the Director of Special Sales, GIRL PRESS, PO Box 480389, Los Angeles, CA 90048.

A percentage of the profits from *Girl Director* will be donated to a nonprofit organization promoting young filmmakers.

Author's Acknowledgements

Just like making a movie, writing this book took the efforts of many people working behind the scenes—so let's roll some credits here. Many thanks and much appreciation to the following individuals and organizations for their assistance, encouragement and support:

Betsy Amster, Teena Apeles (Pogi too!), Liz Barrett, Anne Blecksmith, Kristen Borella, Godfrey Chesire, the helpful staff at the Margaret Herrick Library of the Academy of Motion Picture Arts and Sciences, Jane Cooper, Grady Cooper, Ed Halter, Laura Kim, Erik Leidel, Kiran Perohit, Reina Lauren Platt, Jude Gorjanc, Peyton Reed, Marta Sanchez and Women Make Movies, John Schultz, Mady Schutzman, and all the other folks at CalArts who inspired me to think about writing, women, and film: Nathalie Seaver, Lori Ungemah, Jerry's Video Reruns, Radha Vatsal from the Women Film Pioneers Project, Erin L.Weston.

Special thanks and some sympathy for my family who have put up with cameras in their faces on any and every occasion—Grandma, Mom, Dad, Kara, Drew, Murphy, and the rest—thanks for keeping me supplied with confidence and content. Also my indebtedness to in-house Super 8 advisor and inspiration extraordinaire, Norwood Cheek is gigantic—his D.I.Y. enthusiasm for film is all over these pages.

The super-fun flipbook would not be possible without Director Catherine Hollander and soon-to-be superstar Girl Directors Jessica Petersen, Sydney Townsend, and Raquel Deriane. Thanks to all of them, plus their parents, Iris and Chuck Petersen, Amy Townsend, and Muna Deriane, as well as organizer Leslie Hoffman and, of course, Larry.

Huge gratitude to the Girl Director Production Posse: Amy Inouye, Elizabeth McCallie (Harper Lou too), and Pam Nelson, who not only brought their visionary talents, extreme patience, and good humor to the table, but always had tasty snacks in tow too. Thanks to Amy McCubbin for her research expertise and Natalie Blacker for all of her organizational help. Also, to Kim Gordon and Kimberly Peirce, thank you for your wonderful reviews and eager response. Last, but certainly not least, thanks to Allison Anders for her foreword and for the enthusiasm and support she has generously offered me.

Finally, to each of the directors who gave of their valuable time to talk with me and to add their enormous contributions to this book—thanks for stepping up to the mike to let us in on your moviemaking process.

Andrea, age 3, dreams of the magical world of telling stories on film and video.

Allison Anders
Jane Anderson
Gillian Anderson
Gillian Armstrong
Tina Bastajian
Esther Bell
Lizzie Borden
Gurinder Chadha
Joan Chen
Joyce Chopra
Stacy Cochran
Martha Colburn
Martha Coolidge
Tamra Davis
Katherine Dieckmann
Heather Rose Dominic
Cheryl Dunye
Nora Ephron
Su Friedrich
Rita Gonzolas
Bette Gordon
Maggie Greenwald
Leslie Harris
Kate Haug
Amy Heckerling
Mary Ann Henry
Catherine Hollander
Bronwen Hughes
Sarah Jacobson
Miranda July
Barbara Kopple
Karyn Kusama
Melanie Mayron
Deepa Mehta
Jocelyn Moorhouse
Laura Nix
Yvonne Rainer
Nancy Savoca
Margie Schnibbe
Susan Seidelman
Britta Sjogren
Penelope Spheeris
Helen Sticker
Melinda Stone
Rachel Talalay
Betty Thomas
Irene Turner
Naomi Uman
Agnès Varda
Claudia Weill
Lina Wertmüller

Andrea Richards

Mabel Normand,
silent screen star
and pioneer director.

Contents

1 **Foreword** by **Allison Anders**

2 **Introduction**
Hey, What Is a Girl Director?

4 **Chapter 1**
A Little History of the "Action"
The Pioneer Women Who Started It All

20 **Chapter 2**
Get an Idea and Go!
- ★ Movie Madness—
  Deciding What Type of Movie to Make
- ★ A Smashing Idea, Make a Short!
- ★ Still Searching?
- ★ Movie Types and TV Formats

32 **Chapter 3**
Stuff You'll Need and
How to Get it for Next-to-Nothing
- ★ Finding Your Format—
  Film, Video or Digital Video?
- ★ Getting to Know (and Love) Your Equipment
- ★ Funding Your Flick

42 **Chapter 4**
Make a Movie Solo or Find a Crew?
- ★ Who's My Crew and My Cast and
  What Do They Do?
- ★ Discovering the Many Talents among Us
- ★ Go You Superstar—
  How to Make a Movie with Just You

52 **Chapter 5**
Prepping Your Production
- ★ Writing a Script
- ★ Preparing a Storyboard and Shot List
- ★ Ah, the Perfect Location—Your Backyard
- ★ Set Design without Dollars

62 **Chapter 6**
Putting It "In the Can"
- ★ Learn to Frame
- ★ Hit 'em with Your Best Shot
- ★ Look Out for the Light!
- ★ Calling for Action from Your Actors

76 **Chapter 7**
Finish that Flick!
- ★ Developing Your Film
- ★ An Editrix's Guide to Easy Editing
- ★ Sound Off, Rock Out, or Get Funky—
  Add Music to Your Movie

88 **Chapter 8**
Girl Director, It's Show Time!
- ★ Screening Your Movie
- ★ D.I.Y. Film Festivals
- ★ Spread the Word—Daring Distribution

96 **Chapter 9**
Animate This!
- ★ Flipout Over a Flipbook
- ★ Simply Animated—Stop-Motion Techniques
- ★ Action, Animatrix!

108 **Chapter 10**
Tricks of the Trade
- ★ Low-Tech FX
- ★ Adding Snazzy Sound Effects
- ★ On-Screen Shenanigans

118 **Chapter 11**
Digital Dames Direct!
Making Movies on Your Computer

120 **Endnotes**
Girl Directors Take Over the World—
A Resource Guide

Foreword

by Allison Anders

Well I must admit to being a bit jealous. After all, when I was a girl I didn't know I could be a film director. In fact, I only vaguely knew what a director was. And when I did, it never occurred to me that a girl could be one. But when Andrea called to interview me, I was so excited—it's so cool that girls today will have a resource book to tell them everything I didn't know.

The thing that is so great about girls making movies is this: As females, we have almost no voice on the big screen. Often we find our lives, feelings, and experiences grossly under-represented. Ever go to a movie and leave wondering who on earth that film was made for—'cause it certainly wasn't YOU? Now you have the power to change that.

And that's what excites me about this book—it's specifically designed to help you find your voice, put it on film, and reach an audience—even if it's just your friends at a local club.

What do you make a film about?

Anything that makes you passionate! Maybe you have a really whacked-out group of friends you can shoot endless commentary on. Or maybe there's trauma in your past—film can help you deal with that, heal over it, and help others heal too. Or maybe you have a totally screwed-up family and want to find the humor there—so make a dark comedy. Or, heck, maybe you have a life of happy perfection and would like to see what the *other side* is like—with film, you can do that too.

You see, making a movie is empowering for the director. It is a tool of investigation, a tool for healing and a way to make sense of the world. Ultimately, filmmaking is ***a way for you to take control of your destiny.***

My filmmaking advice? Try to get at the truth. If you find a movie hilarious, it's because it rings true for you. Or if a film makes you cry or makes you think—it's because the filmmaker got at something you found to be true. You have the power to bring that gift to other people. As long as you feel things as deeply as you can, it will show in your work and be meaningful to others.

Watch all of Allison's awesome movies: Border Radio, Gas Food Lodging, Mi Vida Loca, Sugartown, Grace of My Heart *and "The Missing Ingredient" episode of* Four Rooms.

And then there's the FUN of making a movie. I have to tell you that no matter how many movies I make, and with all of the headaches that each one brings, I always leave the experience smiling and deeply satisfied. To me there is no greater fun on earth than making movies.

I know many of you reading this book will one day be a force to contend with. Someday, you'll take all of the big budgets (and big movie stars) away from your big sisters like me. But I look forward to that day, because it will be wonderful to see the films you make about your lives.

So read this book and go make a movie. I can hardly wait to see it!

Allison Anders

HEY—What Is a Girl Director?

What you need to be a GIRL DIRECTOR:

AN IDEA THAT YOU'RE JAZZED ABOUT

COMFORTABLE SHOES

AN IMAGINATION THAT JUST WON'T QUIT

A REFUSAL TO TAKE NO FOR AN ANSWER

A FEW FRIENDS WILLING TO HELP OUT

6 BUCKS & A BORROWED CAMERA

A Girl Director wants to know HOW THINGS WORK, and when she figures that out she wants to be the one who MAKES THINGS WORK, and then, of course, she can't resist making them WORK HER WAY. If she's in a garage, she's under the hood, if she's in a car, you can bet she's driving, and . . . oh yeah, if she's on a movie set, you can be sure she's BEHIND THE CAMERA.

Why? Well, that's where the real ACTION is, and a Girl Director is the chick making the movies she wants to make, telling the stories she wants to tell, and calling all the shots. She's running the show, that's for sure—HER SHOW. That's right, she's got the director's chair with her name on the back, but you'll never find her sitting in it.

BECAUSE IT'S HARD TO SIT DOWN WHEN YOUR IDEAS ARE ON THE LINE, RIGHT?

And just who is this flick-making femme, fueled by Milk Duds, a passion for storytelling, and a bit of bossiness? Guess what baby—*it's you.*

You heard me—you with the dirty fingernails and the worn-out video card ($34 dollars in unpaid back dues!). I saw you go postal on the chatty people in the back row of the theater—there's a name for girls like you.

GIRL DIRECTOR.

Yeah, You Ought to Be in Pictures—MAKING THEM, That Is.

Movies, or *moving pictures* as they were called in the old days, are powerful tools of communication. The pictures, stories and people we see on the screen can truly affect our lives. Let's face it—a really great movie can *change* your life. Think of all the screens you watch during an average day. From the local movie theater to television and computers, we're all tuned in and turned on by moving images. Those pictures and stories give us a window into other worlds and new experiences. That's why your favorite movie makes you cry for the 18th time, or makes you laugh until soda comes out your nose, or just makes you THINK about something in a new way. In one way or another, that movie left you CHANGED. Wouldn't it be great if you could affect other people in the same way?

Do you ever think about the people who are behind those kind of movies, making images come alive to entertain, amuse and yes, even educate? They're telling their stories—why not tell yours?

Why let someone else have all the fun?

For getting your message across, or just sharing a series of images you think look cool, moviemaking is a forum with more than enough room for everyone.

So are you going to be a couch potato your whole life, watching OTHER people's stories, or are you ready to take charge and put something of YOUR OWN on the screen? By making a movie, you can show your perspective on a story, a song, an idea, the world, whatever. SO, GIRL DIRECTOR, WHY NOT TAKE YOUR PLACE ON THE SET?

We're all waiting.

Amy Heckerling

"Being a director, I've never stopped playing. From being a kid and playing with my friends, writing stories, and putting shows on in my neighborhood to going to film school, I've never stopped playing—NOW I JUST GET PAID BETTER FOR IT."

AMY HECKERLING

Amy is one of the most successful directors in Hollywood. Movies she's directed include Fast Times at Ridgemont High, Johnny Dangerously *and* Loser. *Not only did she direct her biggest hits—* Look Who's Talking *and* Clueless, *she wrote the screenplays too!*

SIGNS THAT YOU'RE A GIRL DIRECTOR:

1. **Whenever you get an assignment for a project or paper to write for school, your question is always the same, "Can we make a video instead?"**
2. **You don't leave the theater until after the final credits roll, just to be sure you don't miss any part of the movie.**
3. **You get anyone you can—your little sister, your dog, or even your old stuffed animals—to act in a play you just wrote.**
4. **When someone takes your picture you're more interested in the type of camera they're using than how your hair looks.** 3
5. **You've got notebooks full of story ideas.**

6. **You can't read a book without imagining how it could look on the screen.**
7. **You smell like a strange combination of popcorn and Xerox ink (from making copies of your latest script).**

Chapter One

From Victorian Ladies of the 19th Century to Today's Riot Grr

A Little History of the "Action" The Pioneer Women Who Started It All

Women directors have been making movies since the invention of cinema back in the nineteenth century. That's right—long before Hollywood even existed, women were on the front lines of film production.

In a sense, women were *inventing* the movie industry, experimenting with new technology and finding cool ways to use the new "moving image" camera. And then, when the fat cats with big wallets DID move in on the action, women worked in droves behind the scenes. You may not know them by name, but without these film-femme trailblazers the movies as we know them today would not exist.

So why don't we hear more about these amazing women who helped shape the history of the movies?

Many of the accomplishments of early women directors were later attributed to their male co-workers or even assistants. Why? Because people didn't think chicks could make movies. (Jeez, people can be so stupid.) Also, until recently, historians were more interested in what women did in front of the camera than in what they were doing behind it. Thank goodness they've wised up!

Don't be fooled by this demure looking lady—

This former secretary is the hipster great-grandma to all aspiring Girl Directors. Back in the early days of moviemaking **Alice Guy** (pronounced Alice "Gee" with a hard "g") **Blaché,** a French woman, directed hundreds of films—melodramas, gangster films, and horror movies. You name it, and Alice took it on. Most importantly, Alice was the first person to think of using film to tell a story. A short movie she made in 1896, *La Fée aux choux* (*The Cabbage Fairy*), was based on a French fable about a fairy who produces children in a cabbage patch. It is considered to be the first example of what's called *narrative film,* which applies to just about every movie you see today—movies that tell fictional stories. But until Alice's film, no one had even thought of using film for storytelling.

omen Have Been BEHIND THE CAMERA for a Long, Long Time.

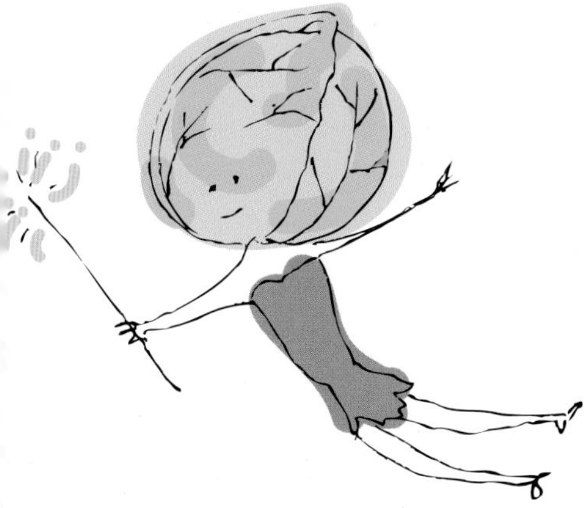

Not only did she create the first story film; Alice was in on the introduction of the talking picture. She made all sorts of early sound movies, which were one to two minutes long and filmed on the *Chronophone,* which recorded sound on a wax cylinder that played along with the filmed images. These films were always ambitious undertakings, and ranged in subject matter from comedies, famous operas, and religious stories to the first cowboy pictures and bullfights.

Alice Guy even made short music films (à la MTV) that featured popular opera singers of the day.

In 1912 Alice Guy Blaché made a science fiction film called* In the Year 2000. *The movie was about women ruling the world. Long before Girl Power, there was Alice Guy!

Some History, Please!

Now you might be wondering: how did this woman get her start in moving pictures way back in the 1800s? Like a true visionary, she saw potential in what other people just couldn't figure out. Alice Guy worked as a secretary in the studio of a famous French photographer, Léon Gaumont. In 1895, Louis Lumière, one of the inventors of the motion picture camera, came to visit Gaumont with his new invention, a contraption that made still photos appear as if they were moving.

Gaumont soon made a movie camera of his own, which was of no apparent use to anyone on his staff—except Alice. She was fascinated. Alice convinced Gaumont to let her experiment with the camera—he agreed, but only on the condition that she didn't let her secretarial duties suffer.

When *The Cabbage Fairy* was screened at the International Exhibition in Paris it brought down the house. Alice's movie "experiment" sold so many cameras that Gaumont realized he was seriously under-utilizing his secretary's talents. From that point on Alice was relieved of her secretarial tasks and given the job of founding Gaumont's filmmaking division. She produced nearly all of the films made by the Gaumont Company for 10 years, and trained some of the future greats of French cinema.

Alice directing a scene at a studio in Paris.

Alice Guy was honored in France as the first woman filmmaker and made a knight in the French Legion of Honor.

Alice building her beloved Solax Studio—at the time, the most powerful moving picture studio in the world.

"We should all realize that whatever we're going through, however hard it is, there's somebody who's gone through it before. There's some woman back in 1915 who wanted to make movies and did. And then there were also many women in 1915 that wanted to make movies and couldn't. And so now we have to do it—because we can't say it's never been done before. We have lots of great women to learn from."

Su Friedrich

(see p. 64 for more on Su)

Alice Guy eventually moved to America. While her husband ran Gaumont's branch office, Alice, ever an independent spirit, founded The Solax Company, her own movie production company. From 1910–1914, Solax made more than 325 movies—35 of which were directed by Alice. In her lifetime, Alice was in some way involved (either as a producer, director, writer or supervisor) in the production of hundreds of movies. So if you're looking for a Girl Director role model, look no further than our beloved Alice Guy. She was just the kind of TAKE-NO-PRISONERS, DO-IT-YOURSELF maverick who ends up changing the world.

"I'd been bitten by the cinema bug."

—Alice Guy

Alice Guy wasn't the only film-femme trailblazer. From the turn of the century to the 1920s women worked in record numbers in the movie business—as screenwriters, editors, directors, and, of course, as stars.

As directors, women in early cinema didn't simply rebel against convention—they had no precedents, no books (like this one), and no mentors. They made up the rules as they went along, and in the process created some amazing movies—some of which still survive today.

When Hollywood Was a GRRLS Town

More women worked in the movie business in its fledgling years than at any other time after, especially as directors. In fact, many famous actresses effectively directed their own films—even if they were not officially credited. Today less than ten percent of directors across the globe are women and women make up only about six percent of Hollywood directors. What a drag!

"Since I learned Dorothy Arzner invented the boom mic, it's been a blast to educate male AND female boom operators about the woman director who invented their job!"

Allison Anders

(see p. 110 for more on Allison)

Call them *film forerunners, producer pioneers* (but don't be foolish enough to think these women ever set foot near a covered wagon, unless they were filming a western)—but whatever you call them, show them some respect. And listen to the message they're sending you from the past: **GIRL, GO MAKE YOUR MOVIE. WE'VE BEEN AT IT FOR YEARS!**

Lois Weber was the first woman to direct, write, produce, and star in a major motion picture.

LOIS WEBER

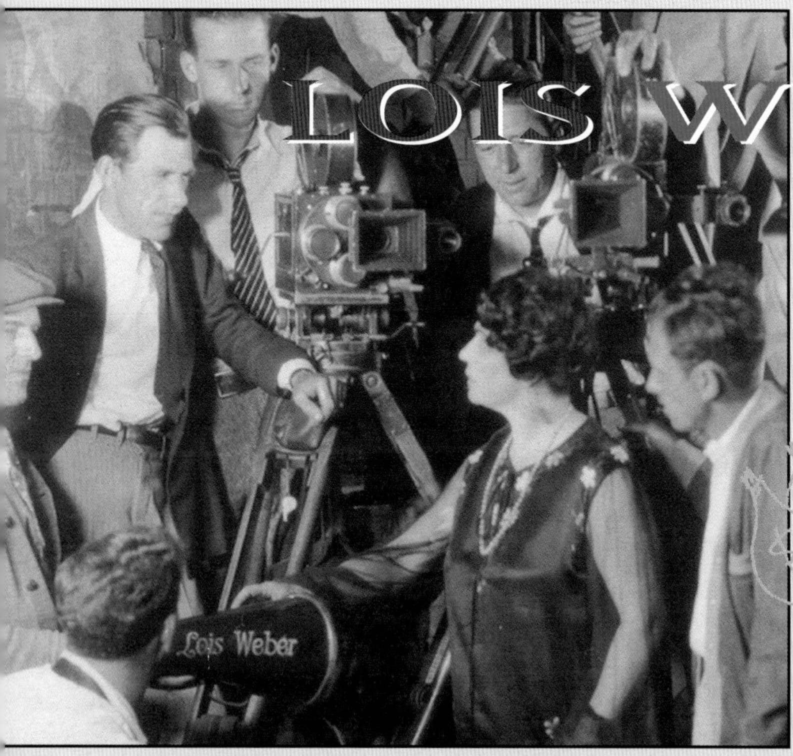

She was a rabble-rouser whose films inspired riots, censorship trials, and even an occasional police raid. And guess what? She was also the highest paid director of the silent era *and* elected Mayor of Universal City, California.

As any good Girl Director knows, there's no better way to get attention than stirring up a little controversy. Especially if you're fighting for a cause (or *causes* in Lois's case) that you believe in with a passion. In fact, passionate outrage is exactly what Lois wanted out of audiences. She understood the power of the movies to change public opinion and used her director's chair as a soap box to spread her ideas—never making a film unless she fully supported its moral stance. Because, for Lois Weber, film was a way to affect attitudes and promote social change—and this former street corner evangelist had no lack of stories she wanted to tell. She took on controversial issues that are *still* touchy subjects today—like birth control, abortion, capital punishment, and racial prejudice.

As the roaring twenties began to rage, jazz age audiences wanted fewer messages in their movies, and, well, *more fun*. Weber's preachy films failed at the box office. She refused to change her serious style and by the middle of the decade suffered a slump in her career from which she would never recover and she lost her company, Lois Weber Productions. The end of her company led her to lose faith in herself and she suffered a nervous breakdown. While she did return to filmmaking for Universal, her days of box office bonanzas were over. Allegedly the highest paid director of the silent era died almost penniless—and rumor is that her funeral expenses were paid by an old friend, screenwriter and director Frances Marion.

"I'll never be convinced that the general public does not want serious entertainment rather than frivolous."

LOIS WEBER

Lois had the courage to place her ideals on the silver screen.

His Brand (1913)
Tells the story of a cowboy who brands his wife on her breast (*ouch!*). When she gives birth to a son, the baby is born with the mark of the brand too.

Hypocrites (1914)
Attacked hypocrisy in the modern world—in business, in the church, and in politics. This movie featured a nude girl as *THE NAKED TRUTH*. (Okay, she was probably wearing a body stocking but that didn't stop the censors from demanding that clothes be hand-painted on her before the film could screen.)

Where Are My Children (1916)
Advocated the use of birth control, and was surprisingly well received—it was 1916 after all!

Shoes (1916)
Exposed and opposed child labor.

The People vs. John Doe (1916)
Featured a man who confessed to a murder he did not commit after being interrogated. The message is a clear protest against capital punishment.

Question: WHY MAKE A MOVIE?

Answer: Because a movie can be more hard-hitting than a fist, sweeter than candy, and better for you than vitamins.

Escape from the studio!

Lois was one of the first directors to add realism to her films by shooting on location. Rather than use studio sets she rented furnished homes and other locales and took her productions there. In fact, she talked Universal Studios into buying her an island for $1,200. Then she blew it up for one of her movies.

Other women who got into the moviemaking act early on:

Elocie Gist

Although there were small, African-American film companies in the silent era, you'd have been hard-pressed to find a black *woman* working in the studio. Moviemaking was primarily a province for the white middle class, so people of color were generally left out—unless they were used as actors in *yet another* degrading role. (*Anyone want to play another Mammy or shuffling stable boy?*) The exception proved to be Elocie Gist, who scripted, directed, produced, and exhibited her own films.

Helen Keller

Did you know that among all the other remarkable things she did, Helen Keller also formed a production company? She created Helen Keller Film Corporation in 1918 to produce and star in her own films. Her best known film was *Deliverance* (1918), a docudrama of Keller's life. Acting a bit part in the production is President Woodrow Wilson.

Mimí Derba

Though the majority of her career took place in front of the camera as an actor, Mimí Derba was the first Mexican female director. She directed, produced, wrote, and starred in *Tigresa* (*The Tigress*) in 1917 and organized one of the first Mexican production companies, Azteca Films.

Cleo Madison

Like so many silent film directors, Cleo was also a film star. As she gained status on screen, she became interested in doing work behind the camera as well. Apparently, when Cleo first asked her studio bosses to allow her to direct, they refused. She struck back by misbehaving on the set—a feat she performed so well that the studio soon offered Cleo her own production company. Between 1915–1916 she directed (or co-directed), and starred in nearly 20 films, most of which addressed the rights of workers and women. And like Lois Weber, Cleo wasn't afraid to tackle taboo topics of the day, like unwed mothers and extramarital affairs. Her films, like *Her Bitter Cup* (1916), are remembered today as some of the earliest suffragist classics.

Want to know more about the powerful women of early cinema?

Check out *reelwomen.com,* which has information, bios, and pictures of all the great women directors mentioned here, PLUS a look at the chicks who are shaping Hollywood today. Ally Acker, a filmmaker and founder of Reel Women, is the author of *Reel Women: Pioneers of the Cinema 1896 to the Present.* You can also check out her important work through the Web site or in the series of documentaries made by Reel Women Productions.

The Women Film Pioneers Project (*www.duke.edu/web/film/pioneers.html*) researches the achievements and history of women filmmakers across the globe (as if Hollywood could hold them all). Not only does the WFPP dig up info on forgotten women filmmakers and work to preserve their films, they also make sure the public (that's you) gets to see these cinematic treasures.

"I had seen men with less brains than I have getting away with it and so I knew I could direct if they'd give me the opportunity."

CLEO MADISON

Musidora

Perhaps the biggest star of silent film in France, Musidora was best known for her portrayal of the villainess vampire, IRMA VEP (read the name closely and you'll see that it's an anagram of *vampire*) in the popular

adventure serial *Les Vampires* (1915–1916). But Musidora did more for the movies than wear her sexy black leotard on screen—she was a novelist, a painter, a dancer, a playwright, and a filmmaker. She directed four films through her own production company, most of which were based on novels by her close friend, the famous French writer Colette. These collaborations were shot on real locations and show Musidora's taste for stylistic experimentation.

Zora Neal Hurston

Okay, so being one of the most important and talented writers of the Harlem Renaissance just wasn't enough for the brilliant and beautiful Zora Neal—she wanted to get into the moviemaking act as well. Though little is documented about her career in film, she did move to L.A. in 1941 to work as a story consultant at Paramount Studios. Apparently she attempted to convince studio heads to adapt her novels to the screen—and to let her direct. Unfortunately, the racist attitudes so deeply entrenched in Hollywood prevented Zora Neal from getting behind the camera as a director.

Mabel Normand

Mabel Normand

Funny gal Mabel Normand was the leading player in the comedy film company Keystone Co.—that is until a "Little Tramp" came along. Charlie Chaplin, that "Tramp," starred with Mabel in several films that she directed. In fact, Mabel insisted that she direct *every* picture she acted in and worked tirelessly, both in front of and behind the camera. As a director she handpicked the other actors, assisted in the film's editing, and even performed her own stunts—getting tied to railroad tracks, scaling high cliffs, and jumping into rivers.

Elvira Notari

Between 1906–1930 this busy Italian filmmaker, nicknamed "The General," made about 60 feature films, as well as 100 documentaries and shorts for her own production company, Dora Film. Not only were her films successful in her native Italy, they were extremely popular in the U.S. among homesick Italian immigrants. Elvira's movies pioneered *cinema of the street,* where directors shot their stories on street locations (not in movie studios) using non-professional actors (i.e., regular people).

While shooting a movie in Spain, where women's voting rights were a hotly contested subject, Musidora allegedly took to the bull ring to demonstrate that women were just as brave as men, and so should be allowed to vote.

Olé.

When these two good friends started making movies together, they changed the face of flickers forever. Take a look at FRANCES MARION and MARY PICKFORD:

Frances Marion
The Screenwriting Machine

You could say she was an important screenwriter, but truth be told, Frances was practically THE ONLY screenwriter for Hollywood during the Silent Film Era.

That's not much of an exaggeration—Frances wrote more than 300 films during her lifetime. She also worked closely on the sets of the movies she wrote—some of which were her best pal Mary Pickford's biggest hits. Marion even worked as a stunt person, and directed three movies. Sadly, only one of these films remains today, *The Love Light* (1921), starring (who else?) Mary Pickford.

Aside from being the most prolific screenwriter ever, Frances somehow found time to direct three films, paint, sculpt, play concert-caliber piano, and have four husbands (at different times, of course).

In her faithful screenplay adaptation of *The Scarlet Letter* (a movie that starred Lillian Gish), Frances included directorial details such as the placement of cameras and suggestions for set design. Frances's scripts were unusually thorough. This was a woman who knew what she wanted.

Frances took home two Academy Awards during her career—not bad for a gal who was expelled from public school for talking back to her teachers, eh?

THE HOLLYWOOD ALL-GRRL NETWORK:

FORGET SIX DEGREES OF SEPARATION, IN THE GOOD OLE DAYS OF SILENT FILM, WOMEN IN POWER MADE SURE THEY LOOKED AFTER THEIR GAL PALS—

- MARY PICKFORD ARRANGED FOR THE GISH SISTERS TO GET THEIR FIRST AUDITION AS ACTORS.
- FRANCES MARION GOT HER START IN HOLLYWOOD WORKING AS AN ASSISTANT FOR LOIS WEBER. SHE WAS WEBER'S PROTEGÉE—ACTING, EDITING, AND WRITING FOR LOIS'S MANY MOVIES.
- LOIS WEBER ENCOURAGED MANY OTHER WOMEN STARS TO DIRECT, INCLUDING GENE GAUNTIER, DORTHY DAVENPORT, AND CLEO MADISON.
- WHEN LOIS WEBER DIED PENNILESS, FRANCES MARION PAID THE FUNERAL EXPENSES.

Frances and Mary were such close pals that Frances even ghostwrote a popular daily newspaper column for her friend under Pickford's name.

"It took longer to make one of Mary's contracts then it did to make one of her pictures."

Producer Sam Goldwyn

Mary Pickford

The other half of this dynamic duo, Mary Pickford, was one of the biggest stars in silent film—in fact, she was the first full-fledged movie star ever. Affectionately called "The Girl with the Golden Curls" or "America's Little Sweetheart" by her fans, the naive and sweet characters Mary played on screen led film audiences worldwide to love her. Off screen, however, Mary was anything but naive. As Charles Rosher, a cameraman, said of her:

> *"She did a lot of her own directing. She knew everything there was to know about motion pictures."*

Mary directed and produced all of her motion pictures after 1920, although she never took screen credit for these roles. Why? Mary, who was well into her 30s at the time, knew audiences still wanted her to be that "little girl" they saw on the screen. So she chose to carefully protect her on-screen persona, guarding her real-life expertise from her public. Even though she looked the part of the innocent, Mary was always a force behind the scenes, orchestrating all aspects of her movies and career.

Mary behind the camera.

Mary and Doug find their studio.

"America's Little Sweetheart" was also one of Tinseltown's most savvy businesswomen. Mary knew the power of her screen presence to draw big box office bucks. She always took care to know the salaries of other big stars (like Charlie Chaplin) to make sure she received the same scale. She wasn't about to let the studios cash in on her talents without giving her a piece of the pie, too. So she moved between studios—often negotiating for higher wages and more control over her films. Before she was 30, Mary was a multi-millionaire.

Eventually, Mary stopped studio-swapping and did something even smarter—she created her own studio, United Artists, with other top stars Charlie Chaplin, Douglas Fairbanks (Mary's husband at the time), and famous director D.W. Griffith. As a studio owner, star, director, and executive producer, Mary had no one but her public to answer to—and that was just the way she wanted it.

Sister Acts

Take another look at that gnarly little sister of yours. Sure, she may drive you crazy, but maybe she'd stop bugging you so much if you let her in on the action. Who knows, once she gets her finger out of her nose and stops dripping Popsicle on your script, the two of you might make a great team, just like these famous siblings—

Lillian & Dorothy Gish

These two big stars of the silent screen got together in 1920 for a movie called *Remodeling Her Husband*. Lillian believed that her sister Dorothy, a great comedian of the silver screen, had never been properly directed. So Lillian took it upon herself to make a film that would fully display her sister's talent. Though this was officially Lillian's directorial debut, she'd been bossing bigwig director D.W. Griffith around for years.

The sisters wanted to make their flick the first all-woman production and tried to hire only women for their crew. (*Pretty cool for 1920, huh?*) They recruited the legendary writer and wit, Dorothy Parker, to write for the film—Parker's first foray into the Hollywood scene. The movie's story centered on a husband who accuses his wife of being too dowdy and unattractive. Dorothy Gish's character is a clever heroine who proceeds to ridicule her husband's notions of beauty and feminine charms. By the film's end, the wife has remodeled her husband's opinion of her, without changing a thing about herself.

Trouble with the cops? Offer them an autograph!

The day before she was to film a complicated scene in downtown Manhattan, Lillian Gish learned she needed a police permit for the shoot. Rather than wait the several days it would take, Lillian decided to shoot the scene anyway. Risking a trip to jail, the film crew agreed to her plan. When the production was discovered by a police officer the next day, Lillian's fame as a movie star paid off. The policeman was a long time fan of her pictures, and allowed her to finish shooting.

Are You the Strong, Silent Type?

Then keep up with the Silent Majority (*www.mdle.com/classicfilms*)! This online journal of silent film has great bios on silent film directors and stars as well as information on film preservation and restoration in their *Lost and Found Film Department*. This is *the* definitive Web site for silent film buffs with listings of live screenings of silent films across the world.

The McDonagh Sisters

Having a big family means you've already got your own movie production team.

At least, that's how the McDonagh sisters turned their home into a moviemaking factory. Between 1926 and 1933 this Australian trio worked together to make four feature films. Paulette was the screenwriter and director, Isobell played all the leading roles, while the last sibling, Phyllis, acted as the production manager and art director. The sisters had an ardent love of cinema and learned most of what they knew about making movies from *watching* them.

Go Ahead, Admit It—

You're hungry for more information on great women directors. Maybe because you're curious, or maybe because you're ready to make your own movie and want to know more about the women who paved the way. Check out these books that splice the chicks back into the history of the pics:

- ***Reel Women: Pioneers of the Cinema,*** by Ally Acker
- ***Film Fatales: Independent Women Directors,*** by Judith M. Redding and Victoria A. Brownworth
- ***The Silent Feminists: America's First Women Directors,*** by Anthony Slide
- ***When Women Call the Shots,*** by Linda Seger
- ***The St. James Women Filmmakers Encyclopedia: Women on the Other Side of the Camera,*** edited by Amy L. Unterburger
- ***Without Lying Down: Frances Marion and the Powerful Women of Early Hollywood,*** by Cari Beauchamp

Women on the Vanguard

Not only did women directors play a critical role in shaping early Hollywood, they were a profound force in creating alternatives to Tinseltown. These were the avant-garde women on the edge:

Germaine Dulac—
The Heart of the French Avant-Garde

Imagine hanging out in Paris during the 1920s among artists, poets, and intellectuals who all sought to express their ideas in new ways. Well, if you were part of this crowd, you certainly would have run across experimental filmmaker Germaine Dulac. Germaine was among the first to take up a camera as a writer might use a pen—to translate the personal point of view of the filmmaker to the screen. For Germaine, movies were an artistic canvas, and making a film was art.

In her pioneering film, *The Smiling Madame Beudet* (1923), Germaine used the camera to show the perspective of the movie's protagonist, a frustrated housewife. The story of the woman's domestic boredom is shown through her eyes as she slowly descends into madness. This masterpiece of silent cinema is the first film to translate a character's feelings onto the screen.

"Here comes Germaine Dulac and her lima bean" was a popular joke that circulated around film-club devotees in France. Umm, why would that be at all funny? Because she made a movie that used time-lapse photography to reveal the slow emergence of tiny plants, one by one, from soil. (More about time lapse on p. 105.)

Maya Deren—

This Russian Jewish emigrant to America was a poet, journalist, and political activist, as well as a filmmaker. In fact, it was Maya who *created* the independent film movement in the U.S. Maya financed her own films, so she was free to experiment with moviemaking in a way no studio would ever permit.

Not only did Maya pioneer many of today's experimental techniques, she also fought to establish alternative distribution and screening venues (like film festivals and film societies). Most of all, Maya wanted people to see movies outside of the box-office mainstream.

Maya Deren, the mother of underground movies.

Cool huh?

Some of Maya's film explorations included collaborating with painters to make *film poetry.* Maya used film to travel to the interior of the human mind to create dream-like or abstract stories on screen.

1895 — The first movie theater opens in Paris, France.

1896 — Alice Guy's *La Fée aux choux* is screened to the delight of the audience. Her employer, Gaumont, sells lots of cameras as a direct response to Alice's film. This film is also considered the first fictional film ever made.

1906 — Elvira Notari begins directing, co-producing, and writing movies. By 1930 she's made more than 60 feature films and 100 shorts.

1914 — Lois Weber's film *The Naked Truth* causes riots in movie theaters and is banned in some states for alleged nudity.

1917 — Marion Wong is the first president of the Chinese–American production company, Mandarin Films. The production company is the first to be staffed entirely by Chinese Americans.

"My philosophy is that to be a director you cannot be subject to anyone, even the head of the studio. I threatened to quit each time I didn't get my way, but no one ever let me walk out." **DOROTHY ARZNER**

DOROTHY ARZNER

She was as brash as the leading ladies in the movies she made, and don't you dare call her Dorothy on the set—it's *Ms. Arzner* to you, please.

Here's how the story goes— She started typing scripts at a movie studio. Then she worked as a "cutter" in the editing room. She wrote and edited big movies. Then she played hardball with her boss for more money and power. She told him she'd quit if he wouldn't give her a directing job—an "A-picture" directing job at that. (She wasn't going to settle for some second-rate movie deal.)

Guess what — her hardball worked. Ms. Arzner got her way and continued to hold her own as the ONLY female director in Hollywood during the 1930s and 1940s.

Dorothy Arzner directed 17 films—most of them huge box office successes. Aside from her creative talents, Dorothy was also known for pioneering cool new techniques. For instance, one day Dorothy suggested to a soundman that he attach a fishpole to the microphone and follow the actors around with it, rather than forcing them to come to stationary microphones to deliver their lines. The *boom microphone* was born—and Dorothy's ingenuity created a device that is still used by moviemakers today.

Dorothy worked with all the major leading women of the day—in fact, her films launched some of their careers. Her eye for great stars was a critical contribution on her part, because the women in her movies were always interesting and strong. That's why the likes of Clara Bow, Rosalind Russell, Lucille Ball, Joan Crawford, Claudette Colbert, and Katharine Hepburn were all happy to work with Dorothy.

No wimpy girls in Ms. Arzner's flicks, thank you!

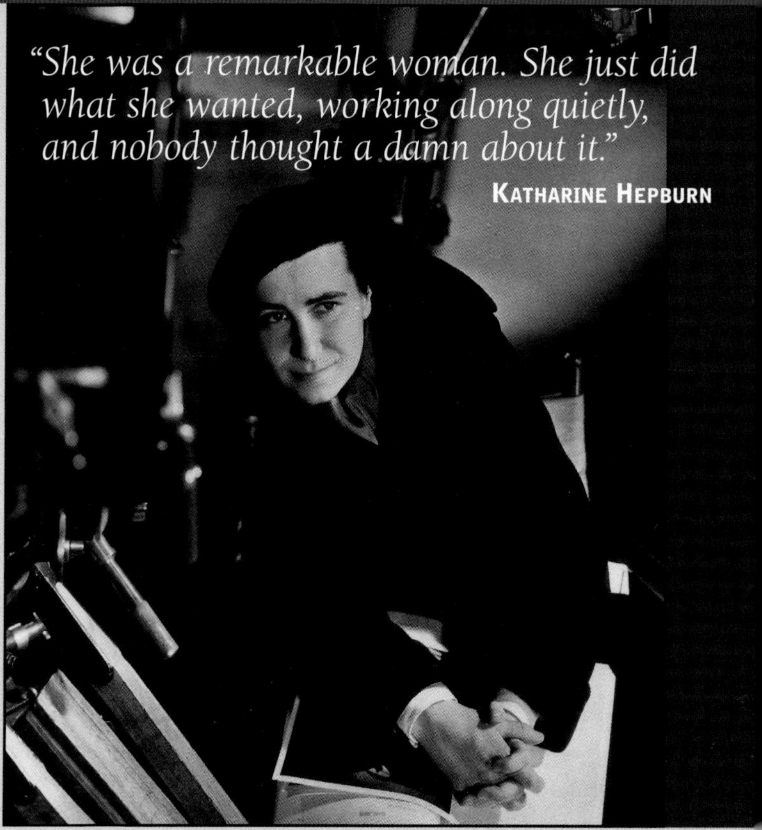

"She was a remarkable woman. She just did what she wanted, working along quietly, and nobody thought a damn about it." **KATHARINE HEPBURN**

MAJOR DOROTHY? During World War II, Dorothy made short films for WAC and trained women to cut and edit these movies. For her work, the U.S. military wanted to make her an honorary Major— Dorothy turned them down. Always a woman to speak her mind, she later said, "I never wanted to be in the Army."

1926 — The McDonagh sisters are the first women in Australia to make a feature film.

1926 — Lotte Reiniger creates the first animated feature film, *The Adventures of Prince Achmed.* The British filmmaker used cardboard, tin, and paper to make her famous silhouette figures.

1929 — American director Dorothy Arzner is the first woman to direct a sound film, *The Wild Party.*

1946 — Maya Deren is the first person awarded a Guggenheim Fellowship and the first woman to succeed as an independent filmmaker.

1949 — Matilde Soto Landeta, the only female director to break into the male-dominated Mexican film industry during its golden age, directs *La Negra Angusitias* (*The Black Angusitias*). Matilde writes, produces, and directs this revolutionary melodrama about an outcast woman who defies tradition to become a leader in the army.

1953 — Kinuyo Tanaka becomes the first Japanese woman director with her movie *Koibumi* (*Love Letters*).

Hold on a Second—Where'd the Rest of the Female Filmmakers Go?

During the silent era, which was roughly from the 1910–1920s, the movie business was in its infancy. No one quite knew just how HUGE (and hugely profitable) movies would become. As the film business became more respectable, the bigwigs moved in—male-run studios that put smaller, independent, women-owned movie companies out of business. Women no longer had the freedom behind the scenes that they had enjoyed for so long. By the 1930s *talkies*—movies that synchronized sound with images—were dominant onscreen. Women directors were pushed out of the film industry—except as screenwriters and stars. Hollywood had become an all-boy playground, except for Dorothy Arzner, the single female filmmaker active in Hollywood at the time.

Ida Lupino

The Dame of the Tough-Guy School of Directing

Like so many other female movie directors, Ida Lupino got her start in the biz as an actor, but she was so bored standing around on sets while "someone else seemed to be doing all the interesting work" that she began directing to fill the time. She founded her own movie production company where she controlled the direction, production, and screenplays of the six feature films they made between 1949–1965. All the while, she continued acting in other directors' pictures, and managed to find time to direct more than 100 television shows.

Like Lois Weber, Ida took on taboo and socially conscious topics that were too hot to handle for other Hollywood studios. Because she owned her own company, she never worried about clearing her subject matter with anyone. So she made low-budget pictures about bigamy, polio, rape, and unwed mothers that elicited both huge controversy and critical acclaim. But unlike Lois Weber, Ida was no preacher—her films rarely had happy endings. Instead, they promoted the bitter wisdom of postwar America, with alienated characters often trapped in nightmarish circumstances. "You name it and we did it," Ida remarked of her harrowing flicks.

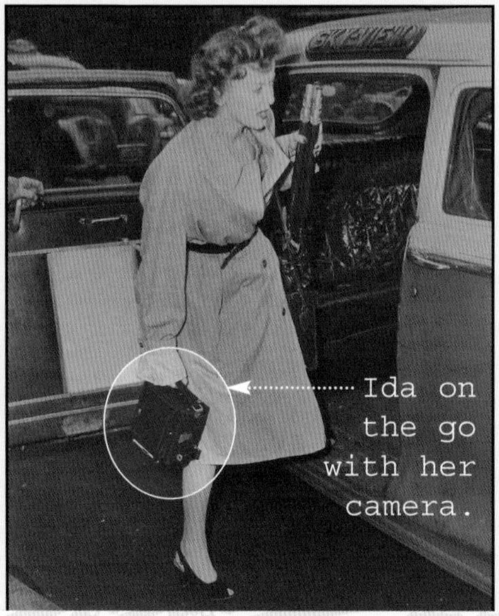

Ida on the go with her camera.

With television's arrival, Ida was given even more opportunities to show off her directing skills. When her company closed in 1954, she became one of the first women to direct for the small screen. Her credits included shows like *Gunsmoke, The Untouchables, Bewitched, The Twilight Zone,* and even *Gilligan's Island.*

1962 Filmmaker Shirley Clarke cofounds the New York Filmmakers Cooperative, a nonprofit distribution company for independent movies.

1975 Chantal Akerman, a Belgian filmmaker, is the first director to work with an all-female crew. Her acclaimed movies include *Jeanne Dielman* and *23 Quai du Commerce.*

1975 Marcela Fernandez Violante, an award winning Mexican director, is the first woman to join the Mexican film director's union.

1976 Barbara Kopple, the director and producer of *Harlan County, U.S.A.* wins an Oscar for Best Feature Documentary.

1976 Italian director Lina Wertmuller is the first woman ever nominated for an Oscar for Best Director.

1983 Barbra Streisand is the first woman to produce, direct, co-write, star (and sing) in a major motion picture in *Yentl.*

IDA was born into a show biz family in London. While she originally wanted to be a writer, she knew her family hoped she'd go into the business, so she did. Per Ida: "My agent had once told me that I was going to play all the sweet roles. Whereupon, at the tender age of thirteen, I set upon the path of playing nothing but hookers."

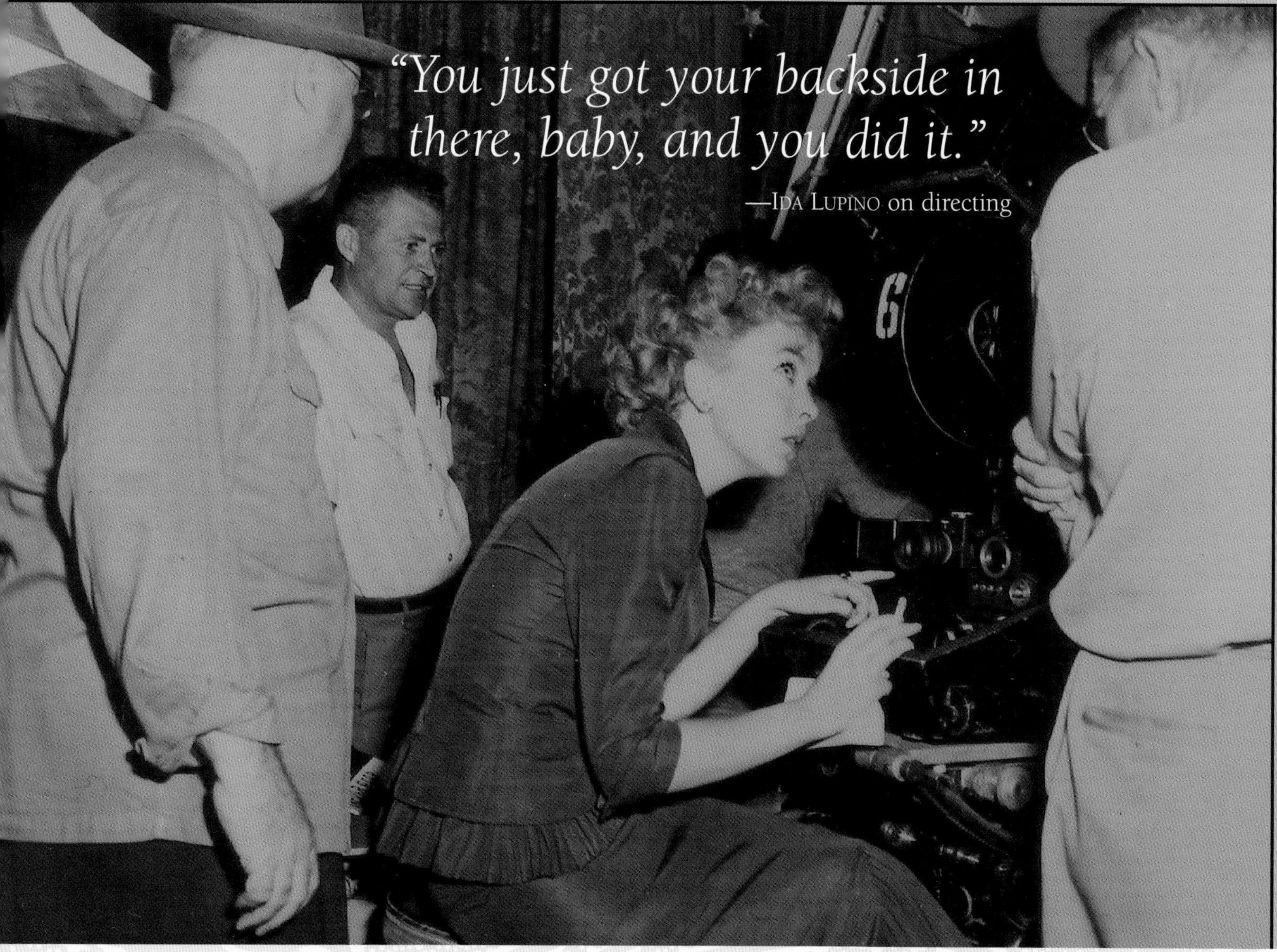

"You just got your backside in there, baby, and you did it."

—Ida Lupino on directing

1989 French West Indian filmmaker Euzhan Palcy is the first black woman to direct a feature-length Hollywood movie with the release of her film, *A Dry White Season.*

1992 Leslie Harris is the first African-American woman to release her own independent feature film. She wrote, produced, and directed *Just Another Girl on the I.R.T.*

1993 Jane Campion, a New Zealand director, wins the Palme d'Or at the prestigious Cannes Film Festival for *The Piano.*

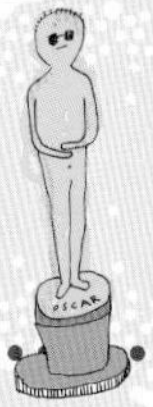

1996 *Antonia's Line,* a Dutch film directed by Marleen Gorris, wins an Oscar for Best Foreign Film—the first for a movie directed by a woman.

1998 For the first time, the films of two women directors surpass the $100 million mark at the box office. The films are Mimi Leder's action-packed *Deep Impact* and Betty Thomas's *Dr. Doolittle.*

TODAY *You picked up this book and started calling the shots to make your first pic!!!*

Chapter Two

Get an Idea and Go!

What Movie Are You Going to Make?

Gangster flicks, action-packed adventures, cartoons, love stories, westerns, documentaries, monster movies, musicals, dramas, travelogues, mysteries, comedies, and sci-fi thrillers—

Whoa, *WELCOME TO MOVIE MADNESS.*

There are so many kinds of movies you can make. It's enough to make the most determined Girl Director dizzy from the sheer POTENTIAL of it all.

Here are a few tips to keep your ideas flowing, and your movie *moving* . . .

Make Your First Movie a Super Short One.

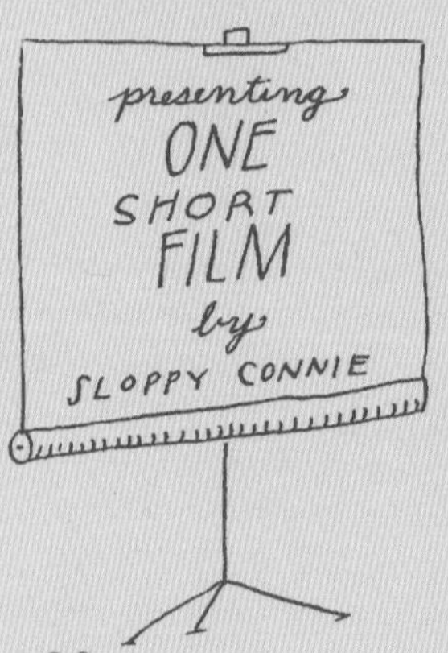

A short film can be anything, but try to keep it under five minutes.

Making a short movie gives you the chance to fine-tune your moviemaking skills without the pressure of producing a three-hour saga. Most directors don't begin their careers by making full-length movies (the two-hour ones you see at most theaters)—they start by making short films, music videos, or even TV commercials.

Because you want your movie to be short, you've got to keep the ideas behind it fairly simple. That means no adapting *War and Peace* or all the *Harry Potter* books to the big screen. Focus on just one subject or scenario, like *girl starts at new school and saves head cheerleader from sadly shallow life.* Or *girl sneaks out late at night and has to talk her way out of trouble*—you get the idea, right?

And remember! This is your first movie, not your *only* movie. So don't feel compelled to cram every good idea you've ever had into one film or video—because believe me, one movie is never enough.

Why It's Hip to Be Short:

- **A short movie** can be made in a day, or even an hour once you get the hang of using your equipment and running the show.
- **A short movie** can be made anywhere—in your bedroom, your backyard, or even on your way to school one morning.
- **A short movie** allows you to see your finished film *really fast* so you can instantly learn from what you're doing. (Rather than realizing that after filming for three hours, you left your camera's lens cap on, or that your main character, a ferocious vampire, actually comes across as one of the nicer Teletubbies.)

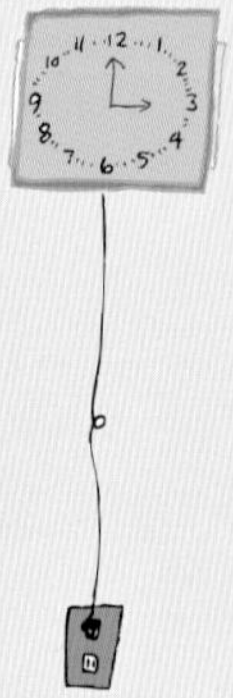

- **A short movie** only takes a single idea.

- Making a **short movie** means you can make a bunch of different movies in the time it would take to make one hour-long film.
- Watching **short movies** is fun. (*Hello,* why do you think music videos are so popular?)

HOW TO GET THOSE IDEAS ROLLING

Yeah, well, join the club. You are *not* a freak if you can't come up with an idea right away. (Or maybe coming up with good ideas is no big issue for you. In that case, Smarty Pants, skip to the next section.) As for the rest of you, here are a few pointers for UNblocking that creative block.

Ideas Come from Anywhere and Everywhere.

Pay attention to your daily life—from reading the Sunday comics to watching your brother smirk at a girl. (*What a dweeb.*) Movie ideas can come from the books you read, the zines you write, the music you make or listen to—even your geometry textbook. If you find yourself bored somewhere, think up movie ideas! Or if you're jamming your brain trying to come up with something—stop straining and start paying attention to the world around you. Before you know it, a great idea will smack you in the face.

Show what you know.
You've got life stories *of your own*—use them! Tell your stories on film or video—your first short could be based on something that happened to you. After all, aren't you the most interesting person you know?

Consult the posse.
Talk with your friends or family about your movie and *listen* to their ideas. Allow them to inspire you. A good conversation generates great ideas.

Keep pen and paper nearby.
You never know when a moment of inspiration is going to strike. Be prepared!

Sweating on the starting line? Here are a few encouraging words from some moviemakers who've been there too.

"There are so many different types of films to make and so many different ways to make them—the only essential thing is to want to make a movie. If you run out into the street with your Super 8 camera, shoot the pigeons, and project it on a building while singing and playing a banjo, you've made a movie."

KATE HAUG

Kate's 16mm films like Deep Creep, The Booby Trap, *and* Pass *screen at film festivals across the globe.* Deep Creep *appears on the* Joanie4Jackie *costar tape,* I Saw Bones.

(see page 72 for more from Kate)

"Make films you care about rather than ones you hope will bring you 'fame.' Life is too short, and filmmaking is too hard to waste energy on something that doesn't feel vital to your being."

BRITTA SJOGREN

Britta won the 1996 Grand Jury Prize at the Sundance Film Festival for her short film, A Small Domain. *The movie was inspired by her 95-year-old friend, Beatrice Hays, who plays the lead role. Britta also wrote and directed the feature film,* Jo Jo at the Gate of Lions.

MUSE THIS!

Waiting for inspiration to strike doesn't mean sitting around twiddling your thumbs. Come on—you could waste your life waiting for an idea to magically pop into your brain. Forget that! Become your own muse by following these handy steps.

STEP #1

DON'T PANIC

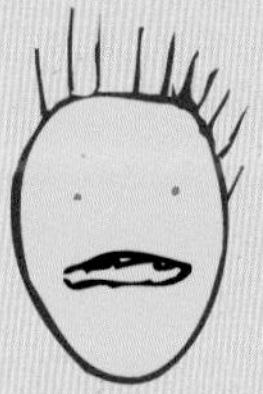

First and most importantly, get a hold of yourself, girl. You can't hold a camera if you're hyperventilating. RELAX and take a moment to think.

STEP #2

MAKE AN IDEA BOOK

If you're going to be a moviemaker, you've got to start thinking *visually*. So as you jot down your movie ideas, imagine how they will appear onscreen. A great way to do that is to make an **Idea Book.** Find a big, no-line sketch notebook where you can write your ideas and cram newspaper articles, magazine cut-outs, photographs, and sketches of anything that catches your creative eye. Draw and doodle all over your Idea Book, make notes around cut-out photos and include all sorts of details—like the color you imagine certain characters wearing, or the time of day events in your movie will take place.

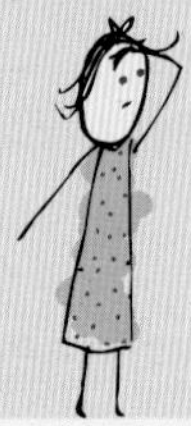

Your Idea Book should be the ultimate moviemaking journal, stuffed with half-hatched ideas and full of all those napkins you've been scribbling on. Let pictures tell stories. It's important that your Idea Book contain more than words—remember the old cliché about a picture being worth a thousand words? *It's true.*

STEP #3

BE A BRAINSTORMER

Set a timer for 5 to 10 minutes and sit down with your Idea Book and your favorite, lucky pen. When the clock starts, scribble down as much as you can, as FAST as you can. Don't stop to judge any of it—just keep writing until your time is up. When it is, your hand should hurt from writing so furiously. Put the pencil down and reward yourself with whatever you fancy (umm, iced coffee and sweets for me!) and move to another place to look it over. Those pages aren't so stark white now, are they? See—you've got some movie ideas after all.

Laura Nix

"Pay attention to the stories in your head. Spend time with these stories. Develop them and nurture them like you would your favorite pet. Your ability to create, refine, and believe in these stories is the most essential starting point."

LAURA NIX

Laura just completed her first feature film, The Politics of Fur*—a comedic melodrama. Laura's films and videos screen widely at art institutions and festivals. She has also worked as the Associate Producer on the documentary* The Celluloid Closet.

"Never give up, even if people don't respond to your project or ideas immediately. Not every movie is for every audience."

KATHERINE DIECKMANN

(see p. 39 for more on Katherine)

STEP #4

KEEP A BACK BURNER HOT

Okay, so maybe you've got the opposite problem, and your Idea Book is overflowing with ideas—all of which, of course, are brilliant. You're stuck, not because you *lack* ideas, but because you have too many. What's a hyper-creative girl to do? Put some of 'em on the back burner!

The back burner is the place where great ideas go to rest for a while, while you work on just one. That will also put them to the test—if your ideas still look good when you come back to them, they're probably worth pursuing.

STEP #5

PAY ATTENTION TO YOUR MOJO & WHEN YOU NEED A CUP O' JOE

Sometimes you need a little peace and quiet to think. Other times you sit and stare at your Idea Book feeling like you're caught in a morgue. If that's the case, then get out into the world—go to a coffee house, a friend's place, somewhere else—anywhere else. Because coming up with your movie idea shouldn't feel like solitary confinement.

STEP #6

NEVER QUIT

NEVER, EVER, AN OPTION.

IDEAS FOR YOUR IDEA BOOK

- Scribble down song lyrics or lines of poetry, and glue images next to them that you like.
- Use your Idea Book as a dream diary, keeping records of all those adventures you have in your sleep.
- Make lists in your Idea Book, because, who knows, maybe writing down what you ate for breakfast will inspire you.
- Gather your friends around and ask each person to place a cut-out object, or a line of dialogue into your Idea Book.

BE A DAYDREAMING FOOL

When you're trying to come up with movie ideas, let your imagination wander aimlessly. Keep your head in the clouds and don't come down to earth until you're ready. When you land back on Planet Production, take pen to paper and try to shape your thoughts into a movie idea you can make *today*.

Agnès Varda

"Don't allow yourself to think it is or will be more difficult for a woman than for a man to become a filmmaker. Just try and you will learn." AGNÈS VARDA

If you'd like to see innovative, independent filmmaking at its best, look no further than the films of pioneer director Agnès Varda. This maverick French filmmaker has been writing, directing, and producing her own strikingly original films for more than 40 years, winning awards and international acclaim. And here's the best part—she started out just like you and me. Agnès made her first film, *La Pointe Courte*, with little money, no film experience, but plenty of enthusiasm and new ideas. "I knew nothing, so I was not afraid," comments Agnès. Her fearlessness was evident in the film's radical structure and original stylistic devices, which heralded a new movement in French cinema. Agnès is often referred to as "the Grandmother of the French New Wave," but remember, this was her FIRST film. "Grandma" was only in her 20s!

***La Pointe Courte* is just the beginning of Agnès's groundbreaking work. She's made countless exceptional movies—shorts, documentaries, and feature films. Her most famous films are *Cleo from 5 to 7*, *Jacquot (De Nantes)*, *Vagabond*, and *Le Bonheur.* Other pivotal works include her documentaries, *Uncle Yanco*, and her most recent film, *The Gleaners and I*. Agnès Varda also controls the business side of her movies through her own production company, Cine-Tamaris. Still, despite her worldwide fame and cinematic accomplishments, she often struggles to secure independent financing for her films. Fortunately, the indomitable Agnès doesn't let anything stand in the way of making great movies.**

Hi Larry!
A featured actor in the even-page flip book (above), Larry the pug (full name: Lawrence Boo Radley Beaux-Beaux Bon Jovi) is our book designer's best buddy and inspiration. He has a degenerative nerve disease which makes the use of a doggie wheelchair necessary. His many vet specialists assure us that he is in no pain. He was once a guest on the *Jim J. and Tammy Faye* television show, and has appeared in the Little Angels Pug Rescue calendar, and the book *Pad*. Larry is currently at work on his memoir, *My Name Is Larry*. He is a Capricorn.

What's Your Movie Style?

MAKE A DOCUMENTARY

Who is the most interesting person you know? Ever wonder what they do all day—in public and private? See if you can follow this person around with a camera and document a "day in the life" of your subject. Then again, your documentary doesn't *need* a human subject—you can follow the family mutt, a stray cat, or an invisible friend (and that's easy since you always get to decide where they go).

Documentaries are usually understood to be nonfiction movies that focus on historical, scientific, social, or environmental subjects (think PBS or the Discovery Channel). But there are other types of documentaries, which focus on people, such as rock stars and politicians. (Think of VH1's *Behind the Music* or A&E's *Biography.)*

So there are lots of different kinds of documentaries, although they do share a few important features. Most docs, for example, are shot on location—meaning that they take place where the subject of the film actually occurred (not in a studio). And they almost always use *real* interviews (rather than actors) to tell a story.

And despite the bad rap, documentaries are hardly boring. After all, there are no boring subjects, just boring storytellers.

Our very own action heroes (stars of our flip book): Raquel Deriane, Sydney Townsend, and Jessica Peterson. Thanks, Girl Directors!

MOCKUMENTARIES: Don't believe what you see!

Some movies use all the techniques of documentaries to tell semi-fictional or completely made-up stories. These **mockumentaries** look and feel like they are documenting real events, but the real people you see on the screen are, surprise, actors! Mockumentaries range from over-the-top parodies like *Spinal Tap* to more convincing spoofs, like *The Blair Witch Project*.

Ideas for Your Dream Documentary

Choose a subject you feel passionately about. Whether it's animal rights or Angela Davis—investigate a subject you care about by making a movie. Think about what makes your subject so fascinating and how you can show that visually on screen.

Pick a subject you'd like to know more about. Find someone who knows a lot about it and ask if you can "shadow" them for a couple of hours with your camera. This is a great way to make a movie, learn something and meet someone interesting.

Choose your favorite woman in history. Make her the subject of a short film. Research her life to prepare your script. You can use photographs and pictures from books as images. Ask a friend to play her and reenact moments from her life. (Who wouldn't want to be Queen Elizabeth?)

Get Grandma going. Document your family history by asking your grandparents or parents to tell stories from way back when. Or try the flip side and interview your little sister about her first day of kindergarten.

Document your fave hobby. If you're a skateboarder, take your camera down to the ramp and film your skater friends and their best moves. Interview them, and intercut that with your "action shots." Expand the movie to include scenes like a trip to the local skate shop for a new board (or even to the hospital if someone takes a tumble).

AND THEN THERE WAS THE TIME WHEN YOUR MOTHER...

Script My Documentary?

Yes, you can loosely script your documentary. In fact, writing down key events you hope to cover before you get into the thick of shooting is a great idea. Having a simple outline of a "script" will keep you focused and ensure that you get the shots you need.

Joyce Chopra

"Be curious about the world, that's the basic thing. Watch people and their behavior. Have a point of view on your material, otherwise you'll just tape and tape and tape with no purpose whatsoever."

JOYCE CHOPRA

More pointers from a pro on how to make an awesome documentary. Joyce recommends you:

- Choose a specific subject that interests you or a question that you want to explore.
- Think about WHY it interests you.
- Make sure these angles are what you film and don't stop until your questions are answered.

Director **JOYCE CHOPRA** *makes all kinds of movies—documentaries, dramas, and, most recently, a movie about girl surfers,* Rip Girls. *Her feature films include* Smooth Talk *and* The Lemon Sisters. *Two of her coolest documentaries are* Joyce at 34 *and* Girls at 12.

These Documentary Divas Rock!

Each of these wildly different directors uses documentaries to give voice to people who often don't have one in the mainstream world—punk rockers, coal miners, radical poets. And they do so on their own terms by financing their flicks themselves. Let's hear it for these relentless risk-takers:

Barbara Kopple
She had a gun pulled on her and pointed in her face while filming her Academy Award-winning documentary, *Harlan County, U.S.A.* But Barbara kept the camera rolling and filmed a coal miner's strike in Kentucky in gritty (and sometimes scary) detail.

Barbara Kopple after filming in a coal mine for Harlan County U.S.A.

Michelle Parkerson
Michelle makes movies she calls "docutainment" about legendary African Americans such as jazz singer Betty Carter (*But Then, She's Betty Carter*), the group Sweet Honey in the Rock (*Gotta Make This Journey: Sweet Honey in the Rock*), and the famous poet Audre Lorde (*A Litany for Survival: The Life and Work of Audre Lorde*). She sums up her approach by saying, "I just want people to discover these artists because they're so fantastic."

Penelope Spheeris
Penelope is best known as the director of Hollywood mega hits like *Wayne's World, The Beverly Hillbillies,* and *The Little Rascals,* but she's also an established name in the world of documentaries. Look for her series, *The Decline of Western Civilization,* which is an ongoing exploration of alienated kids. *Part One* focuses on punk rockers, *Part Two* on metal heads, and *Part Three* on Hollywood runaways. Penelope's docs are as hard core as her subjects—a must-see for aspiring punk Girl Directors.
(see p. 29 for more on Penelope)

Barbara Kopple

"For me the whole essence of nonfiction filmmaking is that it's real. I feel so privileged to walk into other people's lives and have them spill their guts to me—to be able to hear voices that you've never heard before and get into a world you might not know. And then I get to share this with other people, so they too can see and feel what I've been experiencing."
BARBARA KOPPLE

Some of Barbara's other nonfiction movies include American Dream, Wild Man Blues, *and* My Generation, *a film about the three Woodstock festivals. She is also a fiction filmmaker who has directed episodes of the TV shows* Homicide *and* Oz. *She has two feature films in development,* Loving Kindness *and* Joe Glory. *And yes, this two-time Academy Award winner was scared when the strikebreaker held a gun to her head as she filmed* Harlan County, U.S.A. *If you pay close attention to the sound during that segment of the film you'll hear her scream, "Don't shoot!"*

Make a Film that Tells a Fictional Story

Narrative film is a fancy way of describing the kind of movies most familiar to us—the kind that tells a story. Just about every Hollywood movie you see (dramas, comedies, thrillers) are examples of narrative film. You can make and create **your own** story line—it can be funny, thrilling, or tragic—it's all up to you, after all.

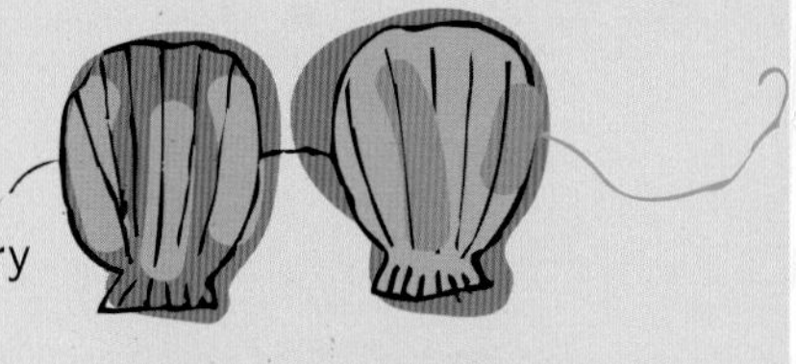

History of the Bra
by Shelly
"It all started with two shells . . ."

"If one is lucky, a solitary fantasy can totally transform one million realities."

MAYA ANGELOU, *writer, producer, and director of* Down in the Delta

Reduce, Reuse, Recycle—
It's Not Just for Coke Bottles Anymore

Feel like you can't possibly come up with an original idea for a story? *Pleeze.* First of all YOU CAN, and secondly, you don't always have to—there are lots of stories that can be endlessly retold in your original way. So don't sit and suffer—try these creative borrowing tricks:

Adapt your favorite short story, comic strip, or urban legend to the screen. Did you know, for instance, that Amy Heckerling's film *Clueless* is an adaptation of Jane Austen's *Emma*?

Remake another film, but add a new ending or mix the characters up—make *Rocky* a female boxer or re-create *Inspector Gadget* from the perspective of the dog. Or tell the other side of the story—like how the Aliens felt in *Aliens 3* or Princess Leia in *Star Wars*.

Pull a genre switch and make a horror film (like *Bride of Chucky*) into a comedy. Imagine Freddy Krueger doing slapstick humor, or someone telling jokes right before their untimely death. Or transform *The Sixth Sense* into a musical!

ADAPTATION IS RE-CREATION

So be selective in what you choose to adapt. After all, novels are not often read in one sitting, so how can one be crammed into 2 hours onscreen? Think about the *essence* of the story and and how to capture it for your movie.

HOW ABOUT GOING EXPERIMENTAL?

Not all movies tell just one story. For that matter, some don't tell a story *at all.* You can express an idea with only pictures and rhythms. Moviemaking is, after all, an art form. So try to think of your movie as a *moving canvas,* adding an image you like here and there to create a cool composition. Anything can look interesting if you get creative: abandoned houses, old colorful bottles, or the clouds in the sky. Once you've assembled your shots, add a song that fits the mood of your images. *Voilà*—a soundtrack! There's no road map to making an experimental film—it's all about *experimenting*, get it?

GO UNDERGROUND!

Experimental movies are also referred to as *underground.* Underground means out of the mainstream, which is why experimental movies are usually not made for commercial purposes (i.e., to make MONEY) but instead to take on taboo subjects that you won't see in the local cineplex.

GET PERSONAL!

Personal movies are about your most familiar subject—YOU. But this isn't just a big ego trip—it's a way to explore your thoughts and opinions in a way that will be interesting to other people.

Dear Diary

Using a video camera to keep a Video Diary of your life can capture the exciting moments in your life (or even the mundane ones) in a completely different way. Record your feelings and commentary on world events, or just your day-to-day life.

Video Diaries are the least expensive movies you can make. Like zines (self-made magazines), they are great vehicles for personal expression AND easy to produce. (Anywhere, anytime!)

Hit the Road

And take your video camera with you! A travelogue movie can document your road trip adventures, whether they're to Singapore or the 7-Eleven store. Think of a travelogue as a record of your observations about your trip. (And if you're REALLY creative, your trip could be all in your head. There's no cheaper vacation, after all, than the one you take in your imagination.)

"Have the guts to tell your stories. When women or girls send me scripts about their personal stories, I tell them it would be so much better to direct the film themselves. There are two big advantages to directing your own story; one, you <u>know</u> the subject better than anyone else, and two, you're the one who can stand up for it."

Lizzie Borden
(see p. 77 for more advice from Lizzie)

MORE GIRL DIRECTOR TIPS

Clear some space for your studio.

Whether it's a drawer, a desk, or a makeshift table, you need to have a place of your own to work. Developing your movie ideas requires somewhere to sit and think. So make yourself a spot where you can write down your thoughts. You don't need a mansion—just a drawer for stuff like your Idea Book or movie journal. At some point you may want to add a telephone so you can call friends (*crew help!*) or find equipment (*Hello, Goodwill?*). Claim a work-space in your bedroom, basement, garage—wherever you can squat—as long as it's private. So make sure it's a place where you won't be distracted by your friends, family, or the TV.

Think big, but take the long view.

Sure, you've got big ideas (that's great!), but start small and give your moviemaking skills time to grow. Don't agonize over your idea for too long. Stop judging and start shooting! Just make it and see what comes out onscreen. YOU WILL MAKE MISTAKES. And guess what—you're not the first. All the greats do, and they learn from them—just like you will.

Always begin with passion.

Start with an idea you love and want to make into a movie, then do it. Pretty basic, isn't it?

MUSIC VIDEOS

Whether you're into hip-hop, heavy metal, or easy listening, you can make a music video that gets down. Pick your fave tune and interpret the song visually by shooting a montage of images—and presto!—you've got a short movie. Making a music video can be even more fun if it's for a band you know. (Better yet, if it's for your own band.) That way, you'll gain experience working with performers. And hey, they might even pony up the cash to pay for the video!

Your music video could be anything—a series of random images, or a specific story inspired by the song's lyrics. There's no science to it—just grab your boom box and camera and get started.

And even though music videos are short, they're a great way to teach yourself about the entire moviemaking process. Since most songs last less than four minutes, you've got a limited amount of screen time to fill. Instant editing!

REEL ROCK
PENELOPE SPHEERIS

"I never considered not being a film director once the idea got in my head—I just went for it. Nothing would stop me. I worked for 25 years trying to be a film director before I had 'box office success'—I was borrowing money from family members just before I directed 'Wayne's World'."

Penelope on the set with a star from The Little Rascals.

Before she made Hollywood mega hits like The Little Rascals *and* Wayne's World, *or her critically acclaimed documentary series,* The Decline of Western Civilization, *Penelope Spheeris was making music videos. She was into music and punk rock rebellion, and so started her career there—producing promotional films for bands. She created the first film production company for music videos in Los Angeles, appropriately called Rock n' Reel.*

"I came up with the concept, I did sound, I shot one camera—I did it all. Of course there were other people helping me, but technically I knew filmmaking from start to finish, inside and out. And I learned it doing those music videos. Later on as a director on feature films, if someone said, 'I'm sorry we can't do that,' I would always stop and say, 'You know what, I know you can and this is the way you do it.' "

"There are tons of influential female music video directors. And there's a whole wave of girl rock stars. They have the power to be real trailblazers for directors. They all kick butt."

BRONWEN HUGHES

(see p. 37 for more on Bronwen)

Wanna make cool cartoons or awesome animated movies? Move on to *Animate This!* Page 96.

Talkin' 'bout Some TV Formats

OKAY, YOU'VE GOT AN IDEA YOU LOVE. GIRL, IT'S TIME TO GO.

Of course, we can't ignore the most-watched medium in the good ole U.S of A.—TV. Television has plenty of room for visionaries like you. Let's explore a few boob tube formats here:

Talk Shows

Grab a mike and start hosting *your own* show. Think about it—don't you know more about the issues that matter to you and your friends than Jenny Jones? Gather your own expert advisors—your pals will love being talking heads—and record your conversations. You can even be Martha Stewart (except cooler) and create your own how-to show. Teach your audience how to change a tire, decorate a skateboard, or play a bass guitar.

The Nightly News

Take that seat behind the news desk and report the news that's missing from prime time. Follow the events happening in your 'hood, or in the lives of people you know. You can even hit the beat with your camera to get a behind-the-scenes look at the stories you're covering.

Commercials and Infomercials

'Fess up, it's happened to you before. It's late at night and you're zoning out in front of the TV watching 20 minutes of an infomercial. There you are, wishing there was something else on, when, suddenly, you're tempted to call and order that oh-so amazing garden weasel or food dehydrator at the very low price of $19.95 (in eight easy installments, of course).

Sure, it has something to do with sleep deprivation, but sometimes even the savviest viewers can be suckered. Use the same power of persuasion for your own idea. Create a short movie for a product that doesn't exist, but should. Or you could do a spoof on an ad for something that *does* exist, but shouldn't (SUVs, for example).

One of my favorite examples of this sort of parody is a hilarious infomercial by the Beastie Boys to advertise their album, *Hello Nasty*. In the "ad" the guys from the band are all sitting around in fake toupees and mustaches talking about how *Hello Nasty* will change their viewers' lives forever. I had to watch for quite a while to figure out it was joke, and when I did, I nearly spit out my late-night burrito from laughing so hard.

Public Service Announcements

TV and radio stations both donate a certain amount of air time to Public Service Announcements (PSAs for short) which are commercials, but for a good cause—like the dangers of drug use, the importance of voting, or literacy.

Now it's your turn. Choose an issue *you* feel strongly about and make a short PSA. As you probably know from the PSAs you've seen, they often rely on dramatic imagery (your brain on drugs as a fried egg) or shocking facts (the number of people who die a year from smoking) to get the audience's attention. In your PSA, you can highlight an issue *you* care about—from animal rights to supporting your local library.

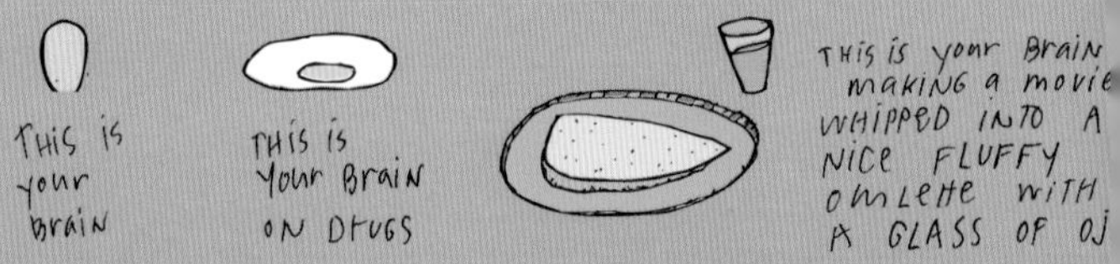

THIS is your brain
THIS is Your Brain ON Drugs
THIS is your Brain making a movie WHIPPED INTO A NICE FLUFFY OMLETTE WITH A GLASS OF OJ

Nancy Savoca

"Everybody has a story—even if you are only seven years old. There's a real power to re-casting your experiences in a movie. Girls are so used to being watched, but as the filmmaker you do the watching. It's great to be on the other side. Girls are ready-made directors!"

Nancy fearlessly and comically explores her Italian-American heritage in films like True Love *and* Household Saints. *Some of her other fantastic films include* Dogfight, If These Walls Could Talk, *and* The 24-Hour Woman.

"A way to not feel like you are totally naked exposing your personal stories is to talk to other people who've been in similar situations and pull from them. Incorporate their experience into your own—the story will still have the same tone, but different details. The story becomes weightier and more universal. And it's more inspiring because suddenly you feel better—hey, everyone is miserable just like you!"

"Girls have a lot to say. In 'Just Another Girl on the I.R.T.' I wanted the girls to be able to express themselves—to let them talk about the angst and problems they are going through. And you know what—the more women and girls we have writing scripts and directing films, the more female characters become real."

Leslie Harris

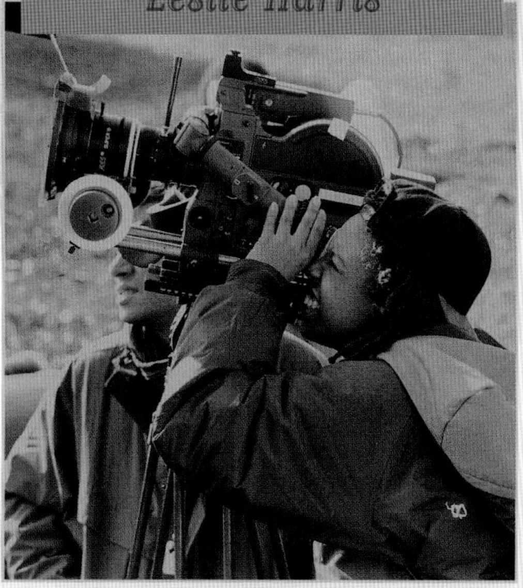

At the end of Just Another Girl on the I.R.T., *the screen reads "A Film Hollywood Dared Not Do." When Hollywood wouldn't back Leslie's first feature film, she directed, produced, and wrote it herself. She did it by volunteering at an art center and using their film equipment for free on weekends. The film was a hit with audiences and critics alike—and Leslie had a full-time directing career.*

"The best time you'll ever have is making your first movie. No one is looking over your shoulder. We forget when we are starting out, we may not have money or support, but we can say what we want to say and DO IT OURSELVES."

Joan Chen

"My first film, 'Xiu Xiu: The Sent Down Girl,' was written by a friend of mine and it was based on a real story about a friend of hers. As I read it, the images stayed with me. When an image stays with you, and the feeling doesn't go away, it's special. It's important to do a story that is significant to you and start out in a very personal way. Do what moves you."

You might recognize Joan Chen from her many acting roles in The Last Emperor, Heaven and Earth, *or in the TV show* Twin Peaks. *Her career in front of the camera began as a teenager in China where the press dubbed her "The Elizabeth Taylor of China." But Joan was so attracted to the story of Xiu Xiu, she decided to get behind the camera to direct and produce the movie. She quickly shot the film on the run in remote grasslands in China and Tibet. Her latest directorial effort is* Autumn in New York.

Chapter Three

Stuff You'll Need . . .
and How to Get It for Next-to-Nothing

Naomi Uman

"I think every filmmaker should:

- own all the tools you need to work
- be able to carry them all at one time
- be able to work wherever you are."

NAOMI UMAN

Naomi Uman lives in Los Angeles and Mexico City where she makes films at a small table, always accompanied by a very small dog.

Okay, Girl Director, now you're raring to go. You call your crew, print out the script, grab your camera on your way out, and . . . *Wait.*

Whaddayamean you don't have a camera? Or some film and videotape? Well, you've come to the right chapter—because this is the one about finding equipment. Here's the bad news: movie equipment can cost kajillions of dollars. That's the way big Hollywood movies are made. Here's the good news: *your* movie equipment will cost approximately nothing. Or at the most, next to nothing. That's because a good Girl Director knows how to work with what she's got—and still make a masterpiece.

What type of equipment do you need? First, you'll have to decide which format movie you want to make. Do you want to use film, video, digital video, or your computer? In a perfect world, you would answer this question, and the magical Film Fairy would deliver your equipment straight to your door.

Yeah whatever.

Welcome back to reality, Director Girl. There is no one-stop shopping place unless you're seriously loaded. And you've got, what—like six bucks? Get ready to do some footwork, girl. It *is* possible to get the stuff you need if you follow the golden rule of low-to-no budget moviemaking:

Use what you've already got or CAN get for free!

First, ask yourself: what sort of equipment do I have access to already? I bet you'll be surprised by how much stuff you can get without selling any vital organs.

ALL ABOUT SUPER 8

If you want to shoot your movie on film (not video) your choice is clear—find Super 8! Sure, there are larger (and more professional) cameras, but those babies aren't cheap, trust me. If you take a film class someday, you'll get to use one of those Big League cameras, but let's stick with the basics for now. Super 8 fits right in with your shoestring budget.

What Is Super 8?

A Super 8 movie camera uses a type of film called, well, Super 8. (Makes sense, right?) Kodak developed Super 8 in the 1960s specifically for home movies. (It's available in color or black and white.) Yep, your grandparents might have used Super 8 to film your parents as snotty little kids. Back then, Super 8 film could record sound as well as images. Sadly, the Super 8 film available today *can't* record sound. That means that your Super 8 movie will be silent, BUT you can always make a soundtrack on an audiotape or play your favorite CD along with it.

What's It Gonna DO for Me?

And here's the really great part: a Super 8 camera, once it's in your hot hands, is going to capture absolutely amazing images on film. And all for less than the cost of a couple of CDs. You can buy or borrow a camera, pay $10 for a roll of film and another $10 for processing, and *BAM*—you've made your movie. And you've made it ON FILM, just like the flicks in the theater (only theirs cost *millions*). That's the beauty of Super 8—it's *film*—the cheapest, smallest format film—but *film*, nevertheless. That's why it is still the standard format for many aspiring directors.

PLUS, with Super 8 you can watch your movies the old-fashioned way, with a real movie projector (also like the movie theaters—only much smaller).

Where Do I GET It?

Tons of Super 8 stuff—cameras, projectors, splicers, and viewers—are hidden away in attics and closets everywhere. A little sleuthing is bound to uncover a Super 8 camera. Since few people other than amateur moviemakers actually *use* Super 8 cameras anymore, they're often tossed out. That's jackpot time for you, my friend.

If you don't find one in your parent's attic, my favorite places to find *cheap* Super 8 cameras are:

- yard sales,
- thrift shops,
- flea markets and junk stores.

But be sure to consult the camera checklist (next page)—you want your camera to actually work. That way you'll spend that 10 bucks wisely.

But before you start thrifting at the local Goodwill or Salvation Army, check in with your own family. Lots of Super 8 filmmakers find their equipment in the attics of parents or grandparents—Grandma's trash is your treasure.

For instance, I am fortunate enough to have a father who saves everything—and I mean *everything*. A trip into my parent's attic could be a weeklong excursion. When I told him I was interested in Super 8, he pulled his old Canon camera from the attic and offered to let me use it. The camera even had the instruction book—a major bonus thanks to my pack rat Dad.

If no one in your family has an old Super 8 camera, you'll have to widen your search. Make a list of everyone you know who might have equipment. Tell the people on your list that you are interested in filmmaking and

SMALL FILM = BIG PICTURES

Check out these Web sites of Super 8 aficionados.

Small movies (*www.city-net.com/~fodder/index.html*) Prepare to be blown away by the cool graphics on this site, including hilarious retro photos and hidden links everywhere. You'll also find up-to-date info on Super 8 film stock, a list of locales for Super 8 services, and a camera guide that features more than 200 models. Plus, don't miss D.I.Y. instructions on editing.

Your hunt for info on Super 8 moviemaking ends with *www.super8filmmaking.com* and *www.super8filmaker.com*. These sites include how-to guides for beginners with abundant info on Super 8 gear, and fabulous odes to the beauty of cheap filmmaking.

Or go straight to the source—film manufacturer Kodak (*www.kodak.com/US/en/motion/super8*) offers a site devoted to Super 8. You'll find info on the Super 8 products and services they sell, a short history of Super 8, and lots of bare-bones advice on shooting the small stuff! And while you're there, check out the main Kodak site (*www.kodak.com*) for the many student filmmaker programs they sponsor.

Look in that attic . . .

> "Your resourcefulness is not about who is going to give you a job—that's too easy. A filmmaker finds what's right outside their window and uses it."
>
> **ALLISON ANDERS**
> *(see p. 110 for more on Allison)*

really want to use Super 8. You'll be surprised how many Super 8 enthusiasts pop up and how willing they'll be to help you.

You might even want to post a notice at your local video store, community center, shopping mall, or camera shop. Post a classified ad in the newspaper, or in Web site chatrooms—get the word out that you're looking for a camera on the cheap.

And don't forget about your school! Some schools even offer film and video classes, or at least have old equipment you can use. Check with the folks at your school to see if they can help, or if they know of another school that has equipment. Ask about borrowing policies and talk to the people in charge of lending—let them know that you're determined.

If you *still* haven't found that camera of your dreams, check the phone book for community media centers—most cities have them to support local film and videomakers. That's you! And finally, your last resort for Super 8 equipment should be camera shops and Internet auctions. Some camera shops resell old cameras, but they're usually very pricey. And many online auction sites (like *ebay.com*) have extensive lists of cameras for sale. Again, they're usually out of the price range of beginning Girl Directors.

Let's Review, Shall We?

To find a Super 8 camera (for cheap!), check the following hot spots (in this order):

1. Attics, closets, and basements of everyone you know;
2. Thrift stores, garage sales, flea markets, and miscellaneous junk shops;
3. Your school and school district;
4. Film groups and nonprofit media centers in your community;
5. Camera stores and online auctions.

or check yard sales.

HEY, DON'T SWEAT THE SMALL STUFF—

Finding a reliable camera is easy if you check this list before you borrow or buy a Super 8 camera:

1. How clean is the camera, both on the outside and inside? I know, I know—here you've found this camera for TWO BUCKS and I'm asking you if it's dust-free. Sure, there should be some wear and tear—just not loads of GUNK (that's a technical term). In particular, be sure to open the slot where the film cartridge fits and check it for strange looking substances (i.e., gunk).
2. Be sure to examine the lens—is the glass broken or scratched? If the camera lens is in any way damaged, don't bother.
3. Check out the battery compartment, which is usually on the bottom of the camera's handle. Open it to make sure that no one foolishly left their batteries in the camera. If they did, it's probably completely corroded (i.e., there's white or green junk all around the old batteries). If there's a lot of corrosion, the camera won't work.

And a final hint, always take a couple of AA batteries with you when you're thrifting for a Super 8 camera. That way you can see if the motor runs before you fork over any cash.

ALL ABOUT VIDEO

You've probably been in pictures all your life—from the tape of your first grade play to the security cameras that record you shopping—nowadays video cameras record your image almost everywhere you go. *Paranoid yet?* Check out the stoplights in your town. At least here in L.A., you're sure to find a small video camera at most major intersections. Speed through a red light and you'll get a ticket in the mail because the video camera has taped your license plate. Take the video camera into your own hands, and turn it back on them!

What Is Video?

A video camera or *camcorder* (that's what we usually call 'em) is basically a camera and videocassette recorder (VCR) in one. Camcorders record motion, color, and sound all at the same time and are extremely easy to operate. Camcorders have a viewfinder (the thing you look through) that acts as a monitor. These days this is usually an external screen attachment, called an LCD monitor. That's the small TV screen that allows you to watch what you've recorded on the spot. That's a BIG advantage of shooting with a video camera instead of a film camera—you don't have to wait until the film is processed, then projected. Video provides immediate gratification. (You can also see your mistakes much faster—better sooner than later, right?)

Currently, there are more than a hundred models of camcorders available, most of which are light and portable (perfect for the gal on the go!). So it's impossible to discuss the specific functions of the camcorder you'll use. But here are some general camcorder characteristics you should know about:

1. **Color.** Camcorders shoot in full color. (Some may also have a switch for black and white.)
2. **A battery pack** (or rechargeable battery). All camcorders run off batteries, which can be recharged from an electrical outlet or car adapter.
3. **Sound.** Camcorders contain a built-in microphone that allows you to record sound and images simultaneously. This is great for catching dialogue, conversations, and interviews.
4. **Auto-Everything.** Camcorders make life easy because everything is automatic, including exposure and focus. What does that mean? Well, that the camera adjusts *automatically* to the lighting and focuses its lens *automatically* on the subject you're recording. That happens by just pointing the camera in the right direction and pressing the *Record* button. The simplicity of "point and shoot" means you don't need a lot of technical know-how to operate the camcorder. Easy, yes. The greatest thing ever, maybe not. But we'll get into the drawbacks of auto-everything in Chapter 6.
5. **Zoom lens.** With the touch of a button, you can control how close you get to your subject without taking one step.

Regardless of which camcorder you use, you can be sure it will sport lots of buttons and special features. Be sure to read the manual and learn where everything is.

What's It Gonna DO for Me?

That's easy—with a camcorder you can make movies with color AND sound simply and cheaply. And here's the real kicker—camcorders record on videotapes that are *reusable*. Yep, you can record over unwanted material on your tape forever. One tape = unlimited takes!

"You have to really, really, really, really, really want to do it. You have to want to do it so bad, you'll die if you don't."

AMY HECKERLING on the most important thing you need to make a movie. *(see p. 3 for more on Amy)*

Can't find a camera? There are still ways to make a movie. **See page 116 for camera-less movie ideas. Or learn to direct from your desktop computer, page 118.**

Where Do I GET It?

Given that every Jane and Joe Schmo seems to have a video camera these days, it shouldn't be too hard for you to track one down. Ask around! Someone in your circle of family and friends is bound to own a camcorder. Take note of which parents bring camcorders to school events (they'll be the ones whose kid is completely ignoring them) and go make pals with them *fast*. Most importantly, convince them that you are capable of using their camera responsibly.

Borrowing someone else's camcorder is a big deal so be respectful of the equipment and grateful to the lender. (Maybe you could offer to tape their next birthday party or event!)

Since many public schools have video and media programs, see if you can enroll in a class (or at least gain access to their equipment). If not, see if you can start a class by talking to your teachers.

And as mentioned in the Super 8 section, don't forget to check the phone book for media centers with equipment you can borrow!

To find a camcorder, check these places first:

- Everyone you know;
- Your school and school district;
- Video groups and nonprofit media centers in your community;
- Educational programs sponsored by Public Access channels or big companies that make video cameras (i.e., Sony or Panasonic).

First Films by the Big Shots

Hey, everyone starts somewhere, right? And before these women were famous movie directors they were scrawny froshes just like you. A few of our director advisors on their very first films:

"A Super 8 remake of 'Dr. Jekyll & Mr. Hyde' that I directed and starred in (as a victim) for a public school media class—which I thought I would never admit to under threat of bodily torture."

—Bronwen Hughes

"My very first film was a group video we did in 8th grade as an extra credit U.S. History project—a very cheesy silent 'Life of Abraham Lincoln,' if you can believe that."

—Irene Turner

"The first film I ever shot was in high school, with this plastic Super 8 camera my grandparents received as a give-away for looking at real estate in Florida. I spent weeks shooting scenarios with my best friend, but when I sent the film in for development it came back black! The camera was a dud."

—Helen Stickler

"I made my first film when I was 8 in an after school animation class. It was stop-motion shot on Super 8. The film was called 'Visitors from Mars' and it's about some aliens that come to earth in a flying saucer and get scared by a tractor with giant bloodshot eyes."

—Margie Schnibbe

"We didn't have amateur video then, so I shot it on Super 8. I was very inspired by George Lucas's film 'THX1138' so I made a weird technical movies supposedly about space ships communicating with its inhabitants."

—Penelope Spheeris

"The first thing I ever shot was a very dopey faux documentary called 'Moonrock.' It was a pretty funny thing that I would not consider watching again."

—Stacy Cochran

"My first video was a short called 'Low Technology' about a 70-year-old man who built a homemade bicycle, painted it yellow, called it THE BANANA, and rode it across the country."

—Mary Ann Henry

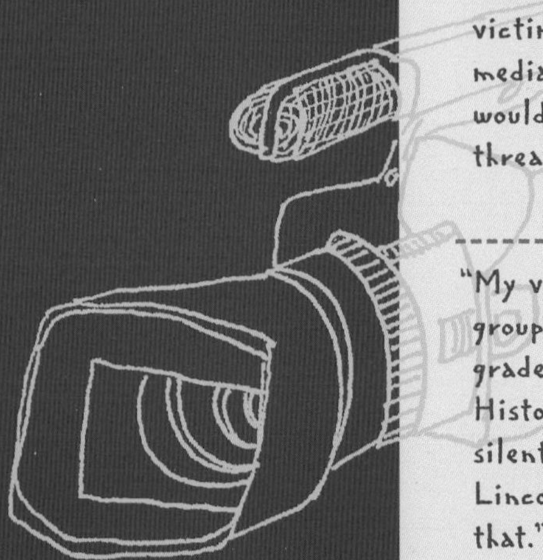

The Digital Revolution

The advent of digital video (DV) cameras is changing the face of moviemaking. Many movies are now shot on DV instead of film. And this revolution isn't only for Big Shots with deep pockets. As DV cameras get cheaper, more low-to-no budget moviemakers are opting for DV and the humble home computer.

Digital video cameras are the latest and hottest video cameras on the market. They also sport a hefty price tag, so don't abandon that camcorder yet. But hey—a resourceful Girl Director can always find one to borrow, right?

What Is DV?

DV camcorders work just like video or regular camcorders for the most part, recording images and sound on a similar sort of magnetic tape. The difference is that it's stored like computer data—as a series of 1s and Os. *Why should you care?* Because that means you'll get much sharper images and sound. Because it's digital, anything you record can be copied with very little loss in quality. It's kind of like the difference between a vinyl record and a CD—the music on your CD will never deteriorate. Same with a DV—the movie you make will last forever.

What's It Gonna DO for Me?

If you manage to score one, a DV camcorder is going to give you the highest quality video available to consumers today, with broadcast-quality pictures and CD-quality sound. It's the closest you can get to the professional look of TV shows. PLUS, the cameras are as easy to use as regular video camcorders and even smaller *(perfect for those undercover exposés).*

Where Do I GET It?

See video camera and Super 8 advice—be resourceful!

Give Your Camera a Little TLC

Even the least expensive film or video camera is a precision instrument—chock full of complex electronic and mechanical parts. And as a Girl Director, your camera is your everything, so you'll want to keep it clean and working like brand-new.

- If you were lucky enough to get the camera's instruction book, READ IT.
- Keep your camera away from anything damaging, like sand, water, extreme temperatures, moisture, and dirt. Be careful to keep food and drink away from your cam, and even more careful about keeping it away from your younger sibling's greasy fingers.
- Make a *camera care kit*: a toolbox or cardboard box with specialty cleaning supplies for your camera. Your kit should include your camera's manual, as well as other supplies like canned air or a soft cotton shirt for cleaning your lens. *Note: Don't ever wipe off your lens with your hands—you'll get fingerprints all over it and could even scratch its surface. (And, honey, that's irreparable damage.)*

Bronwen Hughes

Know the skinny on your gear.

"If you're going to be a novelist, you need to know the words; if you're going to be a painter, you need to know what paint does. If you're going to be a director, you need to know the language. I take great interest in knowing the technical aspects—not because I'm fascinated with them—but because I want to know the tools at my disposal to bring out the pictures in my head."

BRONWEN HUGHES

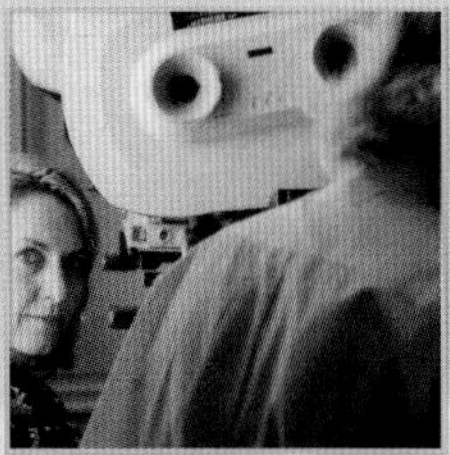

Bronwen is one busy gal, aside from occasionally directing commercials and music videos, her feature films include Harriet the Spy *and* Forces of Nature.

W*oohoo!* **You've finally scored that camera and you're ready to roll.** ***Not so fast.*** **That camera won't do you much good if it's empty. Now you've got to find your film or videotape before you get started on your masterpiece.**

"You have to be resourceful. The idea is the most important thing, not the equipment. Use what you have. Learn to create using any means available."

MELINDA STONE
(see p. 94 for more on Melinda)

That's right, Super 8 makes you smile. Melinda with her new roll of Kodachrome 40 experiences the thrill of fresh film.

Super 8 Film

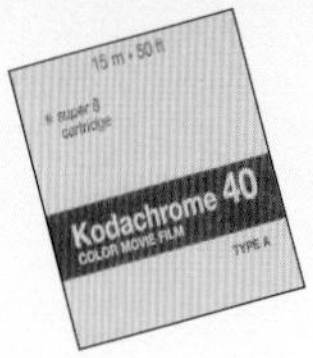

Finding Super 8 film requires a little digging around. Some specialty photo stores and camera shops carry the various types (color or black and white) of Super 8 film stock. The film comes in cartridges that slip into the camera, so loading the film is easy. Each cartridge contains exactly three minutes and 20 seconds of film, so use your footage wisely. If you can't find film in photo stores, order it directly from its manufacturer, Kodak (1-800-621-FILM). Be sure to let the good people at Kodak know you're a student—they give student discounts and are eager to help young filmmakers.

Super 8 film

Video & DV Tapes

The magnetic cassette tapes you'll need to record video can be found almost everywhere, from drugstores and supermarkets to camera shops and convenience stores. Because camcorders are now so popular for home movies, odds are you can purchase a Slurpee and Snickers at the same place where you buy your videotape. Prices vary, but you should be able to find regular camcorder videotape, with two hours of footage, for less than five bucks. DV tapes will set you back slightly more, and they usually include only an hour's worth of footage—but hey, that's a small price to pay for pro-quality goods.

So now you've got everything you need to start shooting: a camera (camcorder, a DV, or fresh-outta-the-attic Super 8) and some film or videotape. But how are you going to WATCH it? Not to worry—here's where we tell you how to get access to that screen, projector, or monitor that will take your film to its audience:

Super 8

In order to watch your Super 8 movie, you'll have to send your exposed film to a lab for processing. Then you have two options: to transfer your film to video using a camcorder or DV camera, or to find a Super 8 projector.

Let's review the first option—transferring to video. *Why shoot on Super 8 if you're only going to switch to video?* Good question. Super 8 film transferred to video *retains the look of film,* even though it's on video. Cool huh? It's also a really quick way to see your film without a projector.

But, if you can find one, it's even more fun to see your film AS FILM—i.e., to screen it with a projector. Super 8 projectors are about 1/4 the size of the projectors used in movie theaters and are really easy to use. And the hands-on experience of threading your own film through the projector can't be beat. You'll get the experience of start-to-finish filmmaking, from shooting to showing your flick.

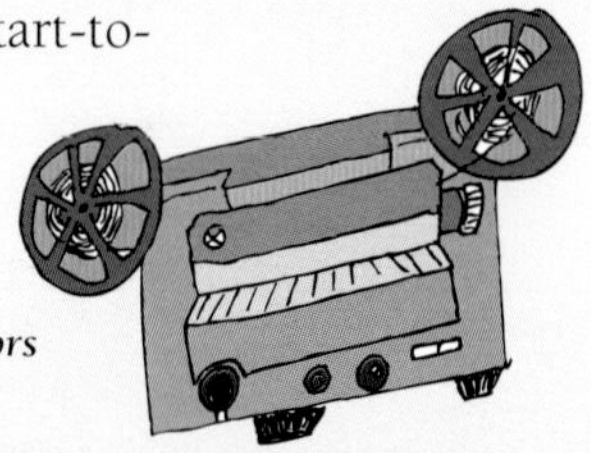

Super 8 projectors

Video and DV

If your movie is on video or DV, your screening and editing equipment will be the good ole' TV and VCR. Camcorders generally hook up directly to your VCR. (If you're using an older camcorder, the tape can go directly into the VCR, just like the movies you rent.) If you're using DV, hook it up to the TV/VCR or to your desktop hard drive, and watch your movie on the computer screen.

And there's just one more thing you might want in order to make your film:

A Tripod

This handy piece of equipment secures your camera and holds it steady while you record your flick. At the top of this funny looking three-legged contraption is a mount, or head, into which the bottom of your camera should screw or fit easily. You'll still be able to move the camera, but your camera movements will be smooth. The trouble with holding your camera in your hands is that even though you *think* you're perfectly still, your arms get jittery (and so does your movie). A tripod will eliminate those unwanted shakes.

But even if you do find a tripod, don't depend on it too much. It is important to practice *hand-held* shots, because you won't always have time to set up a tripod. Don't worry if your hand-held shots make your audience a little seasick for now—you'll get better at keeping the camera steady over time.

Tripods

Getting to Know All About You—

As soon as you find a camera, spend some time getting comfy with it. Hold it and walk around while you look through the eyepiece or at the LCD screen. Move your body around so you get used to the way the camera feels in your hands and how it changes your balance. It's good to learn now how to physically handle the camera so you'll feel secure when you use it for real.

Katherine Dieckmann

Here's the bottom line according to Katherine—

"If you believe in your film enough, believe in it and never waver, it will get made."

Katherine has directed numerous music videos for famous artists like REM, Vic Chesnutt, and Kristin Hersh. She worked for six years directing the TV show The Adventures of Pete & Pete *for Nickelodeon. Her first feature film is* A Good Baby. *She is also writing and directing a feature film based on the real life story of The Shaggs, an all-girl 60s cult band.*

"Every independent director has to find a way to go on with their work. Sometimes you have to compromise in order to do what you really want. 'One for them, one for me,' as Scorsese likes to say." KATHERINE DIECKMANN

$$ FUNDING YOUR FLICK $$

MONEY WOE$

Our esteemed Girl Director advisors agreed on one thing—finding the funds to make a movie stinks. So don't feel alone when you're frustrated with the slow cash flow.

"Money is a real obstacle."

ESTHER BELL

"The most difficult part is financing. All the rest is labor and talent."

MARTHA COOLIDGE

"I hate finding the money."

MARY ANN HENRY

"Here's humble advice—consider your realistic budget."

HEATHER ROSA DOMINIC

Okay, Girl Director, you've managed to sweet-talk your way into the best deals. You've figured out how to borrow instead of buy whenever you can and they know you by name at the *Goodwill*. But inevitably there will come a day when you'll have to pony up some cash. Let's safely assume your cash flow is low—VERY LOW. Short of auctioning off your parents' stereo (would they really miss it, anyway?), how are you going to get the funds to get rolling?

Here's an easy suggestion: Start now by saving money from your allowance or part-time job. If you want to be more inventive, ask your parents (or some other generous adults) if they'd like to act as *producers*. That's a fancy way of asking them to loan you cash. (But hey—maybe they'll be impressed by your know-how.) Or raise money through other fundraising techniques—gather a pool of investors to give you five dollars in exchange for screen credit, or hold a benefit car wash or concert. There are countless ways to raise cash if you get creative.

But it's important that you find the money yourself—that's what keeps your movie *independent* (thus the term *indie film*). The bottom line is that it's YOUR movie when you pay for it. If someone else funds your movie they'll want some control in return. Artistic license comes from financial freedom—nobody's giving away money without strings attached.

BARTER

Every great Girl Director is a master of the fine art of bartering. If you don't have the cash for something you need, chances are you can trade for it. Need equipment rentals or food for your crew? Ask if you can trade services with the people who have it. Offer to volunteer at a media center in exchange for use of their cameras, or tell your friend you'll tutor him in math if he makes sandwiches for your shoot. Who needs cash?

BORROW

Find people who have what you need, and learn how to ask them to borrow it. Sounds easy—but there's an art to this part. Let's say you want to borrow that snazzy camcorder from Uncle Hank—

"Hey Hank—mind if I take the cam out for a spin this weekend?"

probably won't get you anywhere. Hank's not likely to give up his prize electronic toy to someone with a snotty approach like that, is he? But suppose you present yourself professionally to Uncle Hank—perhaps you show him a proposal of your movie project, just to convey your earnestness. Maybe you even offer to put everything in writing with a contract (saying you'll cover the costs if anything happens to the camera). Well, heck, then Uncle Hank wouldn't stand a chance, would he? That camera is practically in your hands.

NETWORK

If you really want to make a movie then you should be TALKING about it, to EVERYBODY. That means going everywhere that other film and videomakers might be—special events, screenings, even chatrooms. You'll be amazed at the willingness of people (strangers, even) to help you out. People are generally very

responsive to excited young upstarts—you could find that perfect mentor!

So go ahead—let people in on your plans and ask for a few favors. If you need help, you've got to ask for it! If you are confident in yourself and excited about your movie your enthusiasm will spread.

NEGOTIATE

Don't rent or purchase anything until you've comparison shopped! That means getting the best deal possible. And always, ALWAYS ask for a student discount.

Speak with retailers about bulk rates for videotapes or film, then persuade your moviemaking friends to join forces and order supplies together. Trade unused products with other film and video makers, and swap labor too. "You work on my film and I'll work on yours."

CHECK THE TRASH BINS

So maybe you and the Fortune 500 part ways on this tip. But I guarantee you'll find lots of gems for your movie in other people's garbage. For instance, a friend of mine found all kinds of film equipment in the dumpster of an elementary school. She took home a camera and a projector, for FREE. (Not to mention a few of those hilarious black and white educational films about getting your period for the first time.)

Keep your eyes peeled for other things you can use—like props, costumes, old lamps, and lumber (for building sets). When your movie is up on screen, no one will know that you found that ape suit in a pile of trashed Halloween costumes, or that you built a space ship from an abandoned washing machine. Looking in unconventional places for what you need means you get to actually *make* movies, instead of just talk about making them.

Most importantly, don't forget to say THANKS to the people who've helped you—with funding, borrowed equipment, or whatever. Be sure to send thank you notes and offer your benefactors free tickets to your movie screening. Or go a step further and list all the folks who helped you in the credits—there's no better thank you than putting someone's name on the big screen.

Make a Budget

Okay, you'd never start a business without a financial plan, and, in many ways, your movie is a small business. So don't start shooting without tallying up your costs.

Possible Expenses:	Estimated Cost	Actual Cost
Camera	Borrowing Sam's camcorder	$0.00 (YAY!)
Film or video tape	$7 for one 2-hour videotape	$5.98 (on sale)
Processing (if you use film)	N/A (using video)	N/A
Editing equipment	Using Mom's TV/VCR	Free
Meals / Food	$20 pizza & cokes for crew	$0.00 (Mom made lunch for us!)
Art for sets / Props	$12 for supplies	$13.15
Transportation costs	None, filming in backyard	Free

Chapter Four

Make a Movie Solo or Find a Crew?

Hey Babe, It's Up to You!

> "It's a privileged hell to direct a movie, but it still makes you crazy."
> **DIANE KEATON**

Did you know actor Diane Keaton also has a respected career as a movie director? Films she's directed include Wildflower, The Girl with the Crazy Brother, Unstrung Heroes, *and* Hanging Up.

So here's the deal: You COULD make your movie all by yourself, but, well, do you really WANT to? Because, as you've probably figured out by now, making a movie involves a lot of work. Even a small film is a BIG production. It usually takes a group effort to get a picture onto the screen. In fact, movies are one of the most collaborative art forms—even lower budget Hollywood movies generally have 20 to 60 people working on the crew. Fortunately, you're *not* making a Hollywood movie, so you'll only have to sweet-talk a few of your closest friends into crew duty. You're the chick in charge, so it's up to you to determine the size of your crew.

Now comes the tricky part: who are you going to choose? Start close to home and ask your friends if they want to get into the moviemaking act with you. Why not surround yourself with your posse on the set? Drafting a few of your good pals will make the workload less overwhelming AND give them the chance to add their creativity to your flick (and save you from a few stress-related freak-outs).

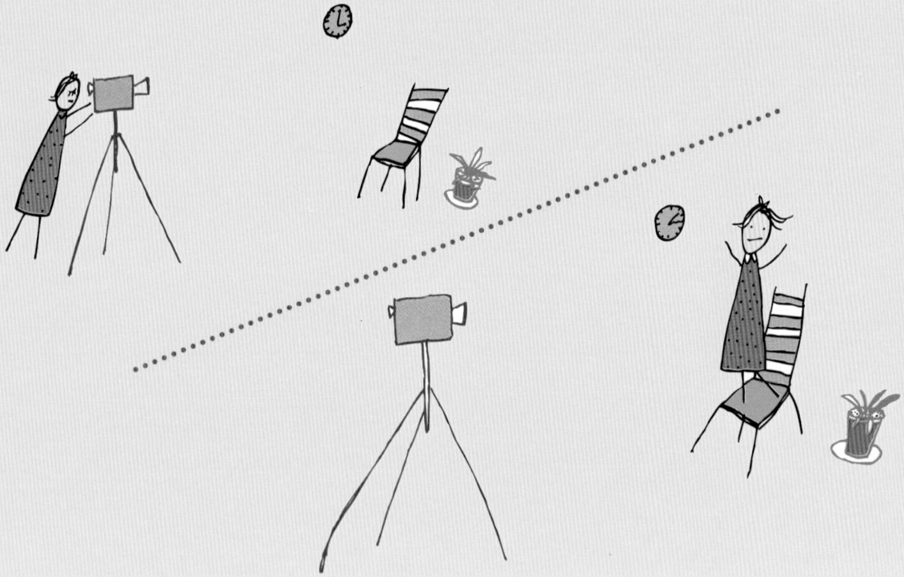

How to start recruiting?

Start TALKING. Tell anyone who might be interested about your film or video project, and THEN tell them that you're looking for production help. If they seem like willing volunteers, tell them their options for getting involved. Since, most likely, your pals will be working for free, it's best to give them a job they'll LIKE.

Who's on Crew?

Some possible jobs for your movie crew posse include:

Art Director
Think of the Art Director as the head diva of set design. She plays a critical role in shaping the overall look of the film. For instance, if you're making a movie about Dr. Frankenstein, the Art Director will be in charge of transforming your pad into a mad scientist's lab. She'll be in charge of building and decorating the perfect scary set. (If she's really good no one will notice that Dr. Frankenstein's equipment looks suspiciously like your chem lab test tubes.)

> **Have an Artistic Eye? Be My Art Director**
>
> Looking for a talented Art Director for tiny-budget short movie entitled *Aliens Among Us.* Must be an original thinker with an eye for authentic detail. Must also be able to transform suburban home into space station. Experience with model making and small-scale construction good, but not necessary. Skills in thrift store-junking and dumpster-diving a plus. All interested candidates please email *girldirector@makingmymovieMYway.com.*

Assistant Camera Person (AC)
The Camera Assistant is the chief sidekick of the DP (see below). She's responsible for everything to do with the camera: loading it with film or videotape, cleaning it, and keeping track of it. She's also in charge of the *shot log,* which is a list of shots recorded for the entire movie.

Assistant Director (AD)
If you're the director, the AD will basically be your right hand on the set. She'll help you with every aspect of production, most importantly keeping it ON SCHEDULE. She'll also be the hardnose who maintains order—which means telling chatty crew members or onlookers to ZIP IT before the cameras start to roll. The AD also takes charge of the more routine stuff—like summoning the cast and making sure everyone (and everything) is in the right spot before shooting starts.

Caterer
(Craft Services)
Hey—this is more important than you think. If you're a small-budget filmmaker, chances are the only thing you're offering your cast and crew is a little free lunch. So be gracious and take this part seriously. Whether it's Chef Boyardee or Captain Crunch, it's good to have someone volunteer to make sure there are snacks and drinks available on your shoot. That's especially true if you're shooting outside—if it's sunny out you'll want to make sure there's plenty of water (and suncreen!).

Cinematographer (DP)
Sometimes called the Director of Photography (or *DP*), the Cinematographer is the *eyes* of your movie. DPs are in charge of how the movie is going to look. She's the person who holds the camera, lights the sets, and frames the shots. The DP is given complete power over the actual image the camera records, and for this reason, I suggest you be your own DP. See, the Cinematographer knows about all the technical aspects of making a movie and getting the right shots—don't you want that person to be *you*?

"Schlepping equipment alone is a big drag!"
TINA BASTAJIAN
(see p. 99 for more on Tina)

"Follow your dreams. All you need to do is to find that one person who believes in you. And get her to help."
SARAH JACOBSON
(see p. 49 for more on Sarah)

"Collaborate."
Yvonne Rainer
(see p. 66 for more from Yvonne)

Editor

If you plan on editing your movie after shooting it, you might want to bring an Editor on board. Of course, I think you should try it out yourself first. Editors take over when shooting is complete and put together the final movie by organizing footage and selecting the right shots. Basically, the Editor decides *what* scenes and takes will be used, and *how* they'll be used. That means she'll decide when to put scenes in, how long they should be, and in what sequence they'll fall. Editors working the old fashion way—on film—are also called "cutters" since they *cut* actual film to organize and construct the story. If you're using Super 8, find an Editor who has great manual dexterity, because Super 8 frames are tiny.

On Hollywood movies, the Gaffer usually has an assistant called a Best Boy—even if the Best Boy is a chick. How lame is that!?

Gaffer

Sounds goofy, huh? Stop snickering. The Gaffer (if you've got one) is in charge of lighting and electricity. She works with the DP to make sure there's a source of electricity everywhere you need it. That means she's securing all the cords—for lamps, cameras (if they don't have battery packs), and even the coffee maker. In big shoots, the Gaffer is the head of a whole corps of electricians.

Producer

In Hollywood, the role of the Producer can vary widely, depending on the movie. But for your low-to-no budget flick, we'll keep the description more general. And *generally*, the Producer is second only to the Director in the development of the movie. The Producer organizes basically EVERYTHING—especially the funding and budget of the flick. (*Mom, I've got a great investment opportunity for you . . .*). But she's also the person responsible for finding equipment, scouting locations, and recruiting the crew. (*Jessica, I've got a great internship opportunity for you . . .*) Since there's so much for a Producer to do, she usually finds a Production Manager to help out. If that's the case, the Producer's main responsibility is to *watch the money.* That means figuring out how to get the stuff the movie needs without breaking the (tiny) budget. Once shooting starts, the Producer supervises the shoot and sometimes gives suggestions to the Director.

WANTED:
Producer for Excellent Short Movie

Must be part ambassador, part number-cruncher, and part taskmaster. Looking for someone with solid communication skills, who's especially terrific at convincing people she doesn't know to give up expensive stuff for free. Planning skills of extreme importance. Must also be capable of making quick decisions, while at least pretending to be sure of them. Ideal candidate for this position is capable of creating gold from garbage. Pay nonexistent, but will gain experience working with a first-class (albeit, first-time) motion picture director. All interested parties should contact GIRL DIRECTOR immediately.

If you want to get experience on a bigger film set, being a PA is usually the quickest way to get there. In general, it means taking care of all the unexpected tasks that pop up on a shoot. Once, when I worked as a PA on a music video, I spent the whole day driving around in a small town in Tennessee trying to break the producer's hundred dollar bills. Yep, that was the job. I can't say that I learned much about filmmaking that day, but I learned a lot about the backroads of rural Tennessee.

Production Assistant (PA)

Basically a PA is a gopher, as in go-for-_______ (fill in the blank: donuts/extension cords/rowdy extras). PAs are messengers, runners, and (let's face it) servants on a movie set. That's true, but they're essential to the overall production. Don't underestimate the importance of having someone around to help you carry all your gear. Though it's the lowliest job on the set, PAs are the glue that will hold your shoot together.

Production Manager

The Production Manager, if you have one, takes on many of the tasks doled out to the Producer, like finding the crew and cast, arranging for locations, and planning the days you'll actually be shooting.

Script Supervisor

A Script Supervisor keeps track of the smallest details while you shoot. Is your lead actor wearing a watch on her right arm? Or is it her left? If it's the left, then you'd better make sure it's the left in every scene. When you see a slip-up in a movie, like a character suddenly wearing a hat when you never saw her put one on, you can be sure the Script Supervisor had to answer for it. It's her job to watch those details—like actors' dialogue (they DO have a tendency to stray from the script), costumes, and placement of props.

Soundperson/Music Supervisor/Composer

This one's easy to figure out. The Soundperson is in charge of your movie's soundtrack. If you're making a silent movie, she'll be the one who records an original score or song to accompany your flick. Or if you're using a camcorder and microphone set-up, the Soundperson checks the balance of different sounds (actors' dialogue, ambient noise, passing Mack trucks) and advises the Director on how to handle them.

Stylist or Make-up Supervisor

Got a super stylish friend? Maybe she's the right person to be the Stylist or Make-up Supervisor on your movie crew. The Stylist is in charge of "transforming" the actors into their characters, usually with make-up. Her job isn't simply about making actors look "better," but about more complicated issues like lighting and time of day. In general, she must be sure that the actors show up well on film or tape. Also, Stylists stay on set during the shoot so they can reapply make-up as it wears off. ("Powder please!")

Wardrobe/Costume Designer

With your mini-budget, chances are your Stylist will also double as your Wardrobe/Costume Designer. In that case, she'll also be in charge of the clothes or costumes to be worn by the actors. After a careful study of the script, a Costume Designer talks with the Director and Art Director about how the characters should look, taking into account factors like time and setting.

Writer

It's my humble opinion, Girl Director, that you should write your *own* scripts—at least for your first few short movies. But maybe you have a friend who's got a way with words and is less afraid to face the blank page than you are. So ask this pal to come up with a script for your next flick. Make sure she's thick-skinned though—she's got to be able to deal with your input and changes as you translate her words to images.

Desperately Seeking a Skilled Writer

Movie director seeks smart, creative writer for movie work and development of screenplay. Must be top-notch writer, liberated from clichés and clumsy dialogue. Thorough research skills necessary, as is the ability to develop interesting ideas into movies. Must be both an independent genius and a cheery collaborator. No pay, but screen credit and all the Captain Crunch you can eat.

"Never work with someone you wouldn't want to eat dinner with, because you'll be spending lots of time with them."

CATHERINE HOLLANDER

(see p. 61 for more on Catherine)

Smart & Savvy Tips on Working with a Crew

No Flakes Allowed—And That Means You Too!

Make sure that the people you choose for your film crew understand what you'll expect from them. As the chick in charge, it's your responsibility to delegate tasks, and make sure everyone knows what she needs to do.

Here's the hard part: If someone isn't pulling her weight, ask her to quit. Trust me, your movie will suffer if you don't. Just because there's no money changing hands doesn't mean your movie set should be a slacker haven.

Girl Directors play well with others.

Okay, let's face it: being a Girl Director isn't ONLY about bossing other people around (much as you may like that part). The best directors know that to make a great movie, you've got to find help. Friends will inspire you and family members will give Oscar-worthy performances if you just remember to ask. And even if it's just you and the camera recording the dog, you'll still need *someone* to do *something* for you—even if it's just getting your sister to turn down her new CD.

Girl Directors know how to use power.

Girl Directors accept the responsibility of calling the shots, and they don't shy away from making decisions. But they also know that the best use of power, sometimes, is to SHARE it. It's called ***teamwork***, right, and even though you're the leader you've got to choose your words (and battles) carefully. Listening to other people's ideas will only make yours better—and don't forget to give credit where credit is due. Also, always remember that praise (and good snacks!) wins over a cranky crew much better than criticism.

Girl Directors aren't afraid to ask questions.

This is the first movie you're making, not the last, so allow yourself to make a few mistakes, ask a lot of questions and experiment along the way—that's how a real Girl Director learns anyhow.

Girl Directors don't forget their sistas.

As you gain experience, contacts, and new skills, be sure to help other girls and women along the way. Encourage other Girl Directors, and try to work with as many girls as you can. *That's a little something we call givin' back.*

Director Deepa Mehta is best known for her acclaimed trilogy of films, Earth, Fire, *and* Water. *Her other feature films include* Sam & Me *and* Camilla. *Deepa has also directed documentaries* (At 99: A Portrait of Louise Tandy Murch) *and for television* (The Young Indiana Jones Chronicles).

Tips from Deepa Mehta

- Communicate clearly what you want from your actors and crew.
- Be alert and persevere—believe in what you want regardless of how absurd other folks think it is.
- Know your camera lenses—that way you can talk with your DP.
- Wear comfortable shoes!

REALITY CHECK

Let's be honest—no one will care as much about your movie as you do. That's why you're the DIRECTOR. And as the director, it's your job to motivate your volunteer army of workers to do their best. Here's a helpful hint: temper tantrums generally don't build group morale.

The bottom line is to be gracious to the folks who are helping you—they ARE doing you a favor, after all. Until you can pay them for their work, don't expect them to devote their lives to your movie. Don't even expect them to work for you every Saturday in the summer—maybe just Saturdays in the month of June. Keep your expectations reasonable, and be grateful for the contribution the crew is making to you and your movie.

HEY GANG!
THANK YOU!
DOUGHNUTS
FOR
EVERYONE!

"Surround yourself with greatness. Don't treat your crew as if they are slaves. You need the best from everybody and you don't want people to hold back. Inspire greatness."

BETTY THOMAS

(see p. 75 for more on Betty)

Discovering the Many Talents Among Us

So, Girl Director, you've cobbled together your movie crew with your winning charm, lots of promises, and a few bribes. But who's going to get in *front* of the camera? Now's the time to develop your CAST—the actors and extras who appear on screen. Where are you going to find your talent? Once again, Girl Director, just look around, you already know people with unique talents, so use 'em—

MOO
Skippy

Possible people for your cast include:

1. YOU
2. Your family and friends
3. Those school-play types from Drama Club
4. Actors from local acting schools.

First step: Hold an audition! You'll be surprised at how many people are natural hams, just waiting for their chance to get in front of the camera. It's your job to find the best actor for each part. Many of the roles will be easily cast: your little sister makes a much better "baby alien" than your six-foot-tall best friend.

And don't forget to consider yourself: maybe the only person who's right for the lead role just happens to be *you*. Don't shy away from taking a starring role just because you're running the show—lots of great directors act in the movies they make.

Next step: Rehearse. Run through scenes with your cast before you start your movie shoot. They will appreciate the extra attention and guidance. Plus, rehearsals mean actors will be less likely to mess up when the camera's actually on.

Mom
Dad

"My first films always used my family. I was 15 or 16 and I'd be like, 'Hey Mom, I'm making a movie, I need a Mom.' My sister was constantly in my stuff too. You don't know that they're any good, but your family is willing to act in your movies—and they are cheap and available."

TAMRA DAVIS

(see p. 49 for more on Tamra)

Extra, Extra—Be in a Movie without Speaking a Line!

Extras are members of your cast who appear in your movie, but only in non-speaking roles. They are especially important when you're filming large, group scenes like a party, political rally, or music club. And any time you're recording outside (or in a public space), you should have a few extras on hand to be "passersby." Otherwise your story will look like it's set in some weird deserted space. And that's not good unless your movie *really is* set in some weird deserted space.

If your movie requires a scene with a huge number of extras—A LOT more extras than you have friends, you can creatively "cheat" the shot by taping or filming an audience at a sporting event (like a football game) or a concert. Nobody there will care and you can "edit in" the crowd later.

Okay, now you've got the low-down on the basic jobs that make up a movie's cast and crew. Even if you don't use them in your movie, at least you know what all those credits at the end of a movie mean.

The truth of the matter is, if you *really* want to make a movie, you just need YOU (and a camera). Sure, other people's help will definitely make everything easier. But the DESIRE to make a movie comes first and foremost from inside you. And that's why, if you want to, you can make it happen all by your lonesome.

Lead Your Own One-Gal Show

Making your movie solo means you're a one-girl band playing every instrument in the orchestra. Yep, you're the producer, the director, the writer, the editor . . . well, you get the idea. You'll shoot your scenes, load the camera, lay out the lighting, make script changes (the script YOU wrote), log your shots, and check the sound. AND, when it's in the can, you'll promote your flick so that people will actually come and watch it. You'll be hurling yourself headfirst into the world of no-budget moviemaking. It's a scary trip that will leave you exhausted, but completely exhilarated.

But Don't Forget Your Mentor

Whether your crew is made up of one or 30 people, there's one person you can't do without. (And it's not the guy at the record store who buys back your old CDs.)

I'm talking about a MENTOR. A mentor is a person who inspires you and your creative spirit. She's that hip role model who can help you learn the ropes. Ideally, your mentor is someone you're not afraid to talk to—someone who feels like a kindred spirit. She knows your path because she's walked it herself.

Don't know anyone you can ask to be your mentor? Don't despair, because mentors, like shoes, come in all shapes and sizes. And you've got to spend some time looking before you find the perfect fit.

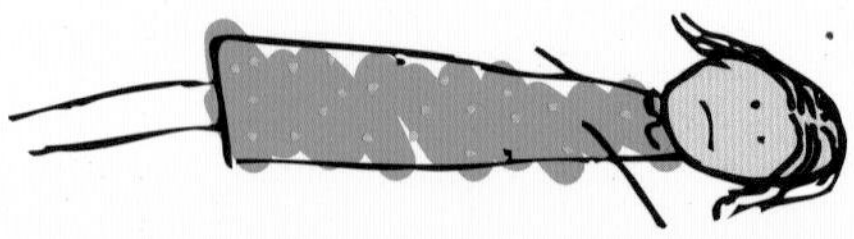

. . . tired

> "Follow your dream, because the person who cares the most wins."
>
> SARAH JACOBSON

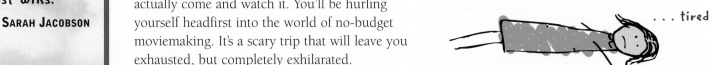

DIRECTOR TYPES:

Women Who Run Their Own Lives

Maybe you don't know anyone who's ever made her own movie, but chances are you know someone with the SOUL of a director. Those are women who aren't afraid to be independent thinkers, to take risks on their own projects, and to be the boss. Some of my favorite examples are Hillary Clinton, Katherine Graham, Kim Gordon, and Oprah Winfrey. I'm talking about indie women who follow their dreams, and DIRECT their lives. You probably even know a few of these powerful types personally. I know I do: my Grandma and my Mom, not to mention a few teachers who showed me how to take charge of my own life.

Directors operate in all walks of life—they publish their own books or zines, start businesses or revolutions, learn to fly airplanes, and, yes, make movies. See, being a director is about HAVING A PASSION and MAKING IT HAPPEN, without waiting around for anyone's permission.

Meeting Your Mentor

Sarah Jacobson

Sarah Says:

"All you need to do is find one person who believes in you—and sometimes you've got to search. Filmmakers are so different than rock stars—they are really approachable. Once I sold copies of my film 'I Was a Teenage Serial Killer' at a zine convention in Los Angeles. I was sitting at this table and a woman came up and asked me what it was. I said 'That's my film that I shot, wrote, directed, and edited myself—and now you can buy it for only $13.' So we started talking about the film and she said something about making her first movie, 'Guncrazy.' And I realized, this was Tamra Davis. Then I completely flipped out telling her how amazing she was and how much I liked her movies. I was so excited to meet another woman director. Since then I've learned so much from her."

SARAH JACOBSON

Sarah is a filmmaker and D.I.Y. distributor. She made her 30-minute film, I Was a Teenage Serial Killer *at age 19. Her feature film is* Mary Jane's Not a Virgin Anymore.

Tamra Davis

Tamra Says:

"When I was 17, I was like all 17-year-olds, pretty full of myself and I thought, 'Wow, I'm just as smart as any of the directors I see making movies.' Now, I'm happy if some girl looks at me and says, 'I can do that too.' I'm waiting for that girl to step in and completely take over. I hope that me and some of the other women directors have been preparing the way for that girl."

TAMRA DAVIS

Tamra makes it a point to mentor other gals who want to be directors too. She has directed many movies, including Guncrazy, Billy Madison, CB4, *and* Skipped Parts. *She's also stayed busy making music videos for bands like* Sonic Youth, Luscious Jackson, *and* Hanson *(the hit video "mmmBop" was one of hers).*

Pictured, at right, with Tamra: Allison Dickie.

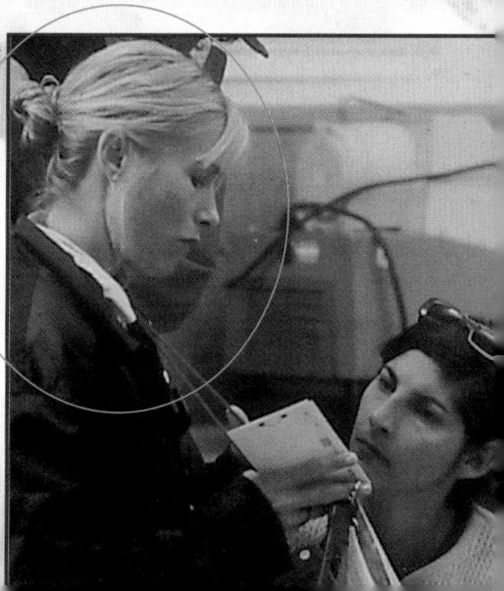

Learn to Speak on the Set by Using In-the-Know Lingo

A-picture

B-picture

A-picture—A term from the 1930s used to describe a higher quality movie on a double feature bill. The lower budget efforts are called **B-pictures.**

ASAP—As Soon As Possible, please!

Cineaste—A French term for *you*—a serious student of filmmaking. A *cineaste* is a devotee of motion pictures (i.e., a film freak!)

FYI—For Your Information.

ACTION!—What you as the director get to SHOUT when you're ready to start recording.

Call Sheets—The list of performers and crew, along with a schedule of *where* they need to be and *when*.

Call Time—The time that everyone needs to be on the set. (That means the crew, cast, and YOU!)

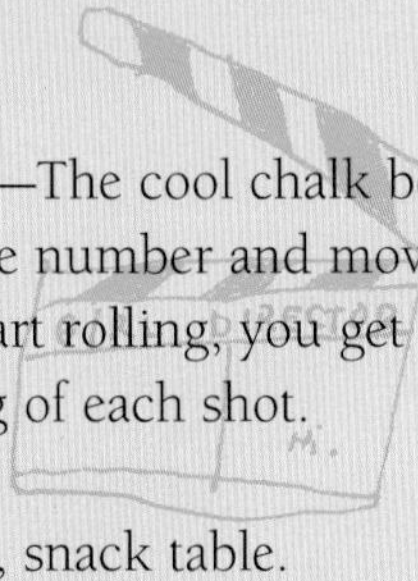

Clapboard or Clapper—The cool chalk board where you write the Take number and movie title. Then, when you start rolling, you get to "clap" it at the beginning of each shot.

Craft Services—Mmm, snack table.

CUT!—The opposite of *Action!* This is what you (the director) yell when you want the film to stop rolling on a scene.

Back to One—This is what you yell when you want to start the scene all over again. As in "CUT! Back to One!"

Day-for-Night—This means that you're shooting during the daytime, but you're making it *look* like nighttime.

Dialogue—What your characters say in your flick.

Dolly—Anything with wheels that can hold your camera. That way you can move IN on, or OUT from the action in a steady motion.

Some things you can use as a dolly are:

- a wheelchair
- a shopping cart
- a skateboard (if you're a real skaterat).

Hand-held Camera—Just what you'd think: this is when you hold the camera free-style, without attaching it to a tripod or any other stationary device. *Keep it steady, girl.*

Honey Wagon—The bathroom, as in "Where's the honey wagon? I've got to go."

In the Can—This doesn't mean you're in the honey wagon! You've got the shot on film or recorded on video, meaning "it's in the film canister."

The Magic Hour—That special time of day, just *before* sunrise and just *after* sunset. It's when there's enough natural light to shoot even though it's not daytime.

Martini—The last shot of the movie.

M.O.S.—Stands for without sound, as in a silent shot, "Are we recording sound for this shot?" "No, it's M.O.S."

Roll Camera!—Another great phrase you get to yell, meaning *Hey, start the darn camera already!*

Setup—Just what you think: the process of getting ready for each shot.

Shot or Take—The basic unit of your movie. A shot or take is the single slice of info you record with the camera—from the time your finger presses *Record*, to when you stop, is a SHOT or a TAKE.

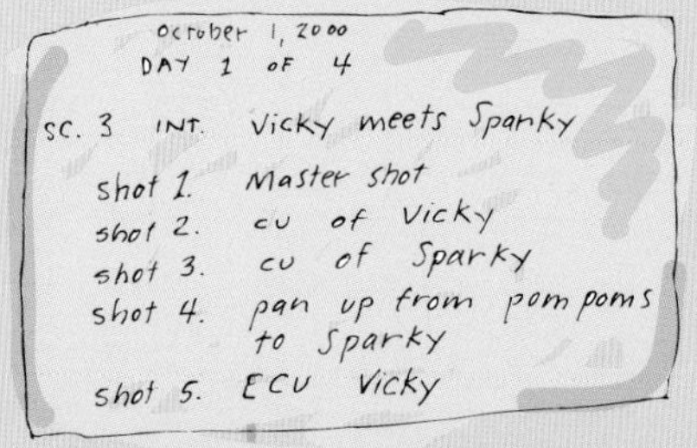
October 1, 2000
DAY 1 OF 4
SC. 3 INT. Vicky meets Sparky
shot 1. Master shot
shot 2. CU of Vicky
shot 3. CU of Sparky
shot 4. pan up from pom poms to Sparky
shot 5. ECU Vicky
Shot list

Scene—A succession of shots. Filming a person looking out the window, then jumping out and flying across the street where she bumps into a dinosaur that's passing by is a *succession of shots*, or a *scene*.

That's a Wrap!—Yay! You're done filming for the day.

GOOD JOB, EVERYBODY. THAT'S A WRAP.

"FYI, this Dolly shot is M.O.S., but the Honey Wagon is in the

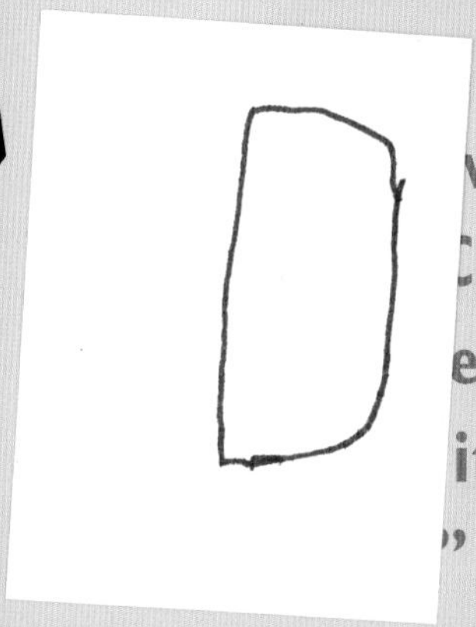

so get ... way ... Craft ... es to ... it ..."

Wassup with the all the funky words— why can't people on a movie set just speak *English*?

As strange as it may seem, this mish-mash of technojargon makes for fast, efficient communication between people working on a movie crew. It's insider speech—and if you want to get inside the movie biz, you've got to know the slang. Walk the walk, and talk the talk, right?

Chapter Five

Prepping Your Production

So here you are, Girl Director: You've got the gear you need, and you've talked a few friends into helping you make your first movie. Your head is crammed with ideas you can't wait to get on the screen. You're raring to go, I know, but now's the time to do your prep work. This is VERY IMPORTANT! That's because PAPER IS CHEAP—cheaper than videotape, and certainly cheaper than film. Spend some time on the steps that come *before* the camera starts rolling and you'll save lots of energy and dough. That means writing a script, scouting a good location, planning shots, and designing sets. So take your finger off that *Record* button, and pay attention to some of these basic prep-steps.

THE POWER OF THE PAGE

Many movie ideas come from the page—a book, a newspaper, a poem, a comic book—anything you read could be the basis of your next film. There aren't any rules to this part—it's basically anything that makes you think: *HEY—this could be a great movie.* As the wheels start turning and your creative process begins, you should start jotting down your thoughts in your *Idea Book.* Then write a simple script. And I stress the SIMPLE part—we're making a movie here, not a novel. Your audience won't be reading your screenplay—they'll be *watching* it. The script is simply a tool for your moviemaking efforts, not your end product. So don't get hung up.

What should a script look like, exactly? Well, it depends. For some moviemakers the script is a fully developed version of the movie, written in a standard format called a *screenplay* (a play written for the *screen*). And for other moviemakers, it's just a vague outline of story events that can be changed once the cameras come on. That's closer to something called a *treatment* in the movie biz. In any case, think of the script as the guidebook to your story. How intricate you choose to make that guidebook is up to you.

"It's very important to prep your movie well and it's the hardest part to get a grasp on. You have to do your prep."

Martha Coolidge
(see p. 76 for more on Martha)

GIRL DIRECTOR, WRITE IT YOUR WAY!

Basically, a script serves as a blueprint for your movie. It clarifies *what* ideas you want on screen, and *how* you're going to get them there. A written script also helps to communicate your vision to your crew and cast. If everyone has a script, you can be sure you're all on the same page—literally and figuratively.

A Treatment

A treatment is a short summary of the events and characters in a movie. It's nothing fancy, and it's SHORT—anywhere from a couple paragraphs to several pages. Writing a treatment is something like writing a VERY short story, except that it's all about the *action*. Treatments usually don't contain dialogue—they focus on the setting and events. There's no standard format for a treatment—it can be a simple list with some text connecting the main action sequences of the movie.

One of the advantages of using a treatment (rather than a full screenplay) is that it leaves you lots of flexibility. It helps you organize your thoughts and plan the sequence of events, but gives you plenty of room to play when the camera starts rolling.

A Screenplay

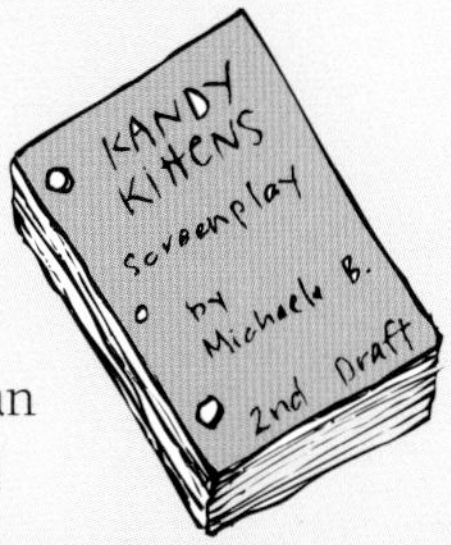

The screenplay is the more common written form behind movies. It's definitely more elaborate than a treatment, and contains all sorts of details—setting, dialogue, time of day, and sound effects, as well as brief descriptions of scenery and stage directions. Screenplays *don't* include details about how the movie will be shot, or camerawork. That's for you, the Director, to do later after you have the script in hand.

Putting pen to paper to create a screenplay will force you to structure the events behind your story, and plan the dialogue for your actors. (That way your lead actor isn't tongue-tied in an important scene.) And note: screenplays usually follow a standard format. That helps other people working on your movie to understand it—producers, actors, and your financiers.

PITCH PERFECT

The simplest treatment you can write is a one-sentence description of your story line. This super-condensed statement is ideal for pitching your idea to other people in a jiffy. For example:

Geeky small town guy goes off to college in the city and has a tough time with his jerky roommates, not to mention rocky romance with a girl who's dating his English professor.

Hey, that movie's already been made. Guess which flick it is:

A. *The Piano* (directed by Jane Campion)
B. *Loser* (directed by Amy Heckerling)
C. *Wayne's World* (directed by Penelope Spheeris)

Answer: Amy Heckerling's Loser

Stacy Cochran

Stacy with her DP Spencer Newman on the set of Drop Back Ten.

"The goal when you're writing is to make the script fantastic and to finish writing. Your obsession is to finish. However, as soon as you finish writing you'll realize that a script is nothing but an UNFINISHED movie. Then you'll be obsessed with the need to cast and shoot it."

STACY COCHRAN

Stacy has written and directed the following movies: My New Gun, Boys, *and* Drop Back Ten. *She also produced and directed a documentary* Richard Lester!, *several other short films, and a* Schoolbreak Special *for TV called* Same Difference.

Tips for Your Script

Mary Ann Henry

"Film and videomakers should be storytellers at heart. Cave paintings were about stories and so are movies. It's common to get caught up in the technology, but you aren't just playing with equipment. You are practicing the art form of storytelling."

MARY ANN HENRY

Mary Ann Henry is the infamous filmmaker behind Chicken Boy: The Movie. *She's made film and video projects for* PBS, The Learning Channel, *and numerous documentaries. She teaches screenwriting and directing and lives on a beach—all while working on two novels!*

1. ***Write Visually.*** Try to paint pictures with your words so you can see the movie as you read the pages. As you write, keep that movie projector or TV screen running through your head. Write down the descriptions of only those scenes that you can see (or hear) on the screen.

2. ***Remember your (limited) resources.*** Sure, it's fun to write a scene in which your lead character grows to be 5,000 feet tall and flattens the U.S. into a pancake—but how are you going to film that? Those are some serious special effects, which your budget probably can't finance. Of course, it can be done, if you're truly determined. But don't make the task impossible.

3. ***Don't forget that a script is equal parts concrete and quicksand.*** Be committed to the words on the page, and yet flexible enough to throw them away when they don't work.

4. ***Listen to your script out loud.*** Stage a reading of it in front of a live audience. Instant feedback can tell you which scenes work, and which don't. You'll also find that your words sound different when they're spoken by other people than they did in your head when you wrote them. Now you can see if you still like them.

5. ***Take advantage of your equipment.*** If you score the use of a waterproof camera (Thank you, swim coach!), write some action around it. Create some underwater scenes in your script—you'd be crazy not to! Or if your aunt comes to town for the weekend driving her superd-up 1930s Studebaker, I'd say your script ought to make use of such a cool prop. You might want to set aside that sci-fi thriller you've been writing, and concentrate on a 1930s gangster flick.

6. ***Cut the clichés.*** If you've heard a line a hundred times before in other movies, don't put it in yours (unless you're poking fun at it). Writing lots of one-line jokes makes a script too cutesy, and when overused they are the ruin of good writing. If you use a one-liner, at least give it some bite.

7. ***While you're at it, strip the script!*** Don't let it get too heavy with dialogue and details. Keep it simple so you can keep your story MOVING.

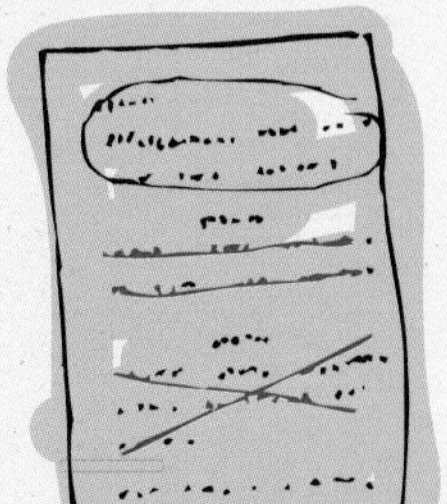

"Scripts are written for the ear, as well as the eye."

MARY ANN HENRY

HERE'S THE STORY—

If you're more of a visual artist than a writer, you might choose to make a *storyboard.* A storyboard is a visual skeleton of your movie, consisting of a series of sketches—usually one sketch per shot. The dialogue is generally printed beneath each drawing. If you think that sounds like a comic book, you've got the right idea. Like a script, a storyboard helps you visualize how the parts of your movie will look and how they will flow together. It's also a good tool for talking to your crew—they can look at your storyboard and get an idea of what you want right away.

You don't need to be an artist to make a storyboard. I've seen (and made) several storyboards that look like drawings by a five-year-old. But guess what—that chicken scratch is all you really need to get started.

SCENES AND SHOTS

The building blocks of your movie will be *scenes* and *shots*. Scenes are basically the various events in your movie—actions that take place during one stretch of time and in one location. Each scene is made up of various shots—every time you start recording or filming you are *beginning* a shot. When you stop recording, you are *ending* a shot. (Between shots you will probably change the camera's position or angle.) Scenes and shots make up a movie!

BREAKDOWN

The first step in making a storyboard is *breaking down your script.*

Start with a blank notecard (or a square piece of paper)—this will be your frame for a single shot. Inside the frame, draw anything important you want in that shot—actions, people, props, locations, or costumes.

Each of the key moments in your movie should be in this storyboard drawing. How many drawings you make depends on the movie you're making, and how thorough you want to be with your storyboard. But be sure to include elements like the placement of actors and props, setting, colors, and camera angles. Draw the image you want the camera to see, and how you want the camera to see it. (From far away? Or from up close?) And don't forget to add dialogue to the bottom of each drawing, if there is any.

MIX 'EM UP

To figure out how best to organize your drawings, move them around and piece them together into scenes. Then lay them out sequentially on the floor around you, or tape them up.

Now take a good hard look at your lovely storyboard—this time with a director's eye. Ask yourself: Will the viewer be able to follow the flow of scenes without getting confused? How is the pacing of events—are you spending too much time on an unimportant event and not enough on the climactic scene of the movie? And be practical! Does your storyboard call for stuff you can't get (like an army tank or a blue whale)? Finally: Will the movie be too long? This would be the time to cut a few scenes, if so.

Your storyboard will also help you spot flaws in your movie, like when a character suddenly surfaces from nowhere or a storyline falls apart. Most importantly, a storyboard will help you "see" your movie for the first time, and put you one step closer to actually making it.

HAS ANYBODY SEEN THE SHOT LIST?

"I always ask myself, what is the one shot I have to have out of a scene or I'll kill myself? Never lose sight of the one thing that excited you and got you interested in the subject in the first place and make sure you get it. In the tumult of making a movie there's so much going on you can get side-tracked—make sure you get the key shots."

JOYCE CHOPRA
(see p. 25 for more on Joyce)

Sometimes your script will be written by someone else, but the storyboard and shot list are always the responsibility of the Director, a.k.a. YOU.

A *shot list* is exactly what it sounds like: a list of all the intended shots for a movie. It's generally created after the script has been written, but *before* the camera rolls. Think of the shot list as the director's "cheat sheet" for the set—only you don't have to write it on the bottom of your shoe. This is where the technical aspects of shooting are described. (We'll explain those technical steps in the next chapter.) The most important elements of a shot list are:

Action / Events in the shot—What's going to happen and who's making it happen?

Location and Props—What's in front of the camera and why is it there?

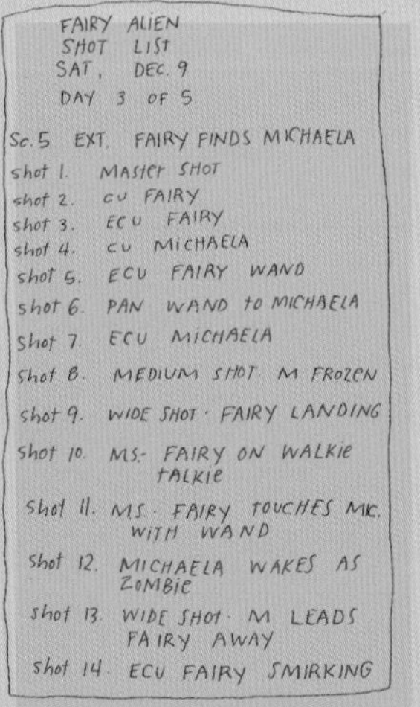
FAIRY ALIEN
SHOT LIST
SAT, DEC. 9
DAY 3 OF 5

Sc. 5 EXT. FAIRY FINDS MICHAELA
shot 1. MASTER SHOT
shot 2. CU FAIRY
shot 3. ECU FAIRY
shot 4. CU MICHAELA
shot 5. ECU FAIRY WAND
shot 6. PAN WAND to MICHAELA
shot 7. ECU MICHAELA
shot 8. MEDIUM SHOT M FROZEN
shot 9. WIDE SHOT · FAIRY LANDING
shot 10. MS.- FAIRY ON WALKIE TALKIE
shot 11. MS · FAIRY TOUCHES MC. WITH WAND
shot 12. MICHAELA WAKES AS ZOMBIE
shot 13. WIDE SHOT · M LEADS FAIRY AWAY
shot 14. ECU FAIRY SMIRKING

Distance from camera to the subject—Is the camera close to the subject or far away?

Camera angles—Are you shooting from a low angle or a high one? From the front or side?

Camera movement—Is the camera stationary or moving around the subject? If it moves—how? By zooming in for a close-up? (Or maybe a tracking shot?)

When your shot list is ready, prepare a *production list*—the stuff you'll need for each shot. This list might include cast, costumes, props, sets, special effects equipment, and any music you want for your soundtrack. You've probably figured out by now that a good director makes LOTS of lists. The more organized you are before you start shooting, the easier your shoot will be. Honest.

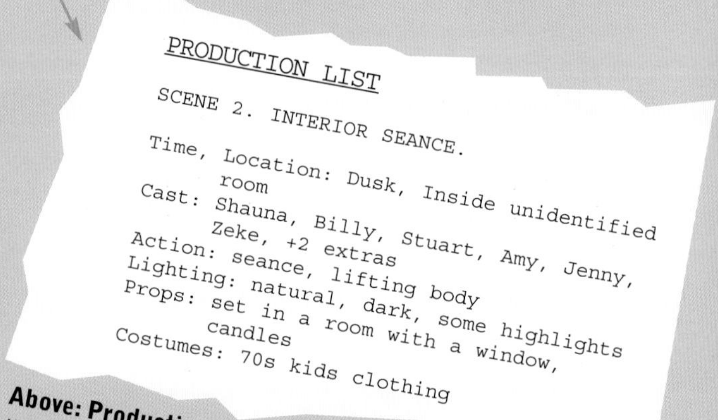
PRODUCTION LIST

SCENE 2. INTERIOR SEANCE.

Time, Location: Dusk, Inside unidentified room
Cast: Shauna, Billy, Stuart, Amy, Jenny, Zeke, +2 extras
Action: seance, lifting body
Lighting: natural, dark, some highlights
Props: set in a room with a window, candles
Costumes: 70s kids clothing

Above: Production list for Catherine Hollander's film, "Light as a Feather." See page 60 for a look at examples of her storyboard, script, shot list, stills from the film, and director's notes.

Margie Schnibbe

"If you don't have some sense of order and discipline you're in trouble."

MARGIE SCHNIBBE

Margie Schnibbe is a filmmaker, writer, and painter whose works have appeared in numerous galleries and festivals. She lives in Los Angeles.

BALI, BELFAST, OR YOUR BEDROOM? WHERE TO SHOOT YOUR FLICK

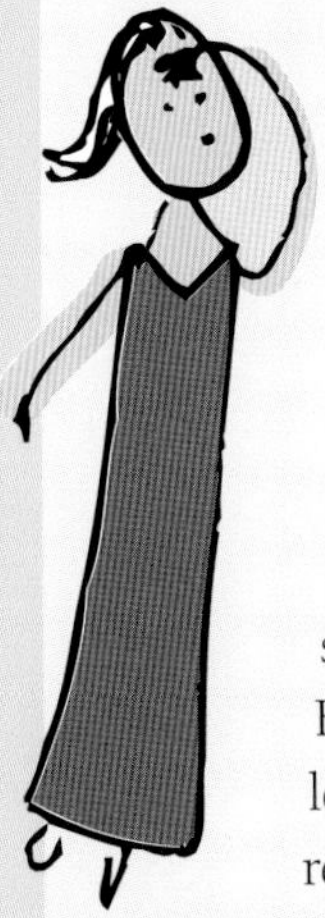

Scouting for location—that phrase sounds more glamorous than it usually is. It conjures up images of helicopters flying over exotic locales, but more often means talking the dry cleaning guy into letting you use his storefront. *(Tip: offer him a credit.)* Basically, your scouting will involve lots of legwork and diplomacy. You'll know you've found the right spot if it seems right for your scene, and if it's FREE. Most people will be willing to let you use their space (i.e., their shop, restaurant, or land) provided you work during off hours, keep out of the way, and don't do any damage.

That last part about breaking stuff is key! Every good director-on-a-shoestring knows that being gracious to people who are DOING YOU A FAVOR is absolutely critical. Not only is it the right thing to do, but it also improves your chances of using their space again in the future. (It also doesn't hurt to get the permission of the owner in writing.) If your shoot is really involved (longer than one day) you'll need to purchase some sort of property or casualty insurance. In general, do yourself a favor and don't shoot around expensive stuff.

For the most part, I recommend shooting in the houses or apartments of people you know, or in public spaces like a park or a beach. Shooting outside during the day is almost always the easiest choice (all natural light!). And never, ever forget: a good location *always* has access to a *honey wagon*. (That's the bathroom, remember?) If not, your crew will be miserable the whole day (and that coffee shop *will* eventually force one of you to buy coffee).

Of course, the easiest place to create your set is in your own home. You don't have to move your equipment, the landlords are friendly, it's free, there's a fridge, and you know where the bathroom is. (*You've just got to keep that primping brother out of there.*) Shooting inside also means you have more control over light and conditions—fickle weather won't shut you down.

Another important element to consider is sound. Beware of locations near major highways and airports, because the background noise will undoubtedly drown out your actors. Plus, the microphone on your camcorder will pick up strong winds if you're shooting outside—so don't try recording on even a mildly windy day.

Last word on locations: don't stage violent fight scenes in an open public space. A passerby might think it's real and freak out. AND NO FAKE GUNS OR OTHER WEAPONS in a public space. That's just *asking* to be hauled away by the police.

Once you find the right location, the rest of your set design will fall into place. You'll know what to build (or move around) to suit your story. Take another look at the script, storyboards, and/or shot list to identify any changes you need to maximize your location.

Location Scouting in Your Backyard

Can't afford to fly five of your closest friends and crew members to South America for your movie's key rainforest scene? Hey, turn on the sprinklers, borrow a few houseplants, and you're in business. The best beginning directors are endlessly resourceful about creating locations in their own backyard.

Set Design without Dollar$

Staying on the RIGHT side of the Law

Here's the one drawback to shooting in a public space: it may require a permit from the town or city. Don't panic. You can usually get one easily (and possibly for free!) by calling the city council. I know what you're thinking—*My shoot is so small I don't need a permit.* That may be true if it's you and a friend with a camcorder. But if it's you and your 20-person film crew taking over a park . . . think again. Without that piece of paper, the police could shut you down fast.

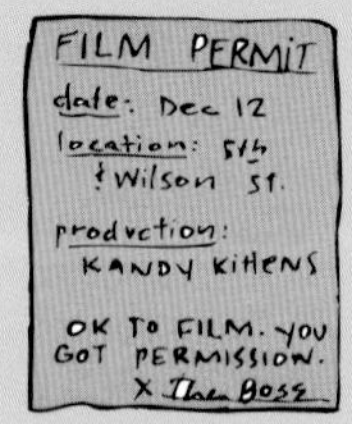

Let's see . . . if you were a big Hollywood production company, you would call in your art department, including your team of set designers, to begin transforming your location into your movie's setting. Those set designers would find everything for you, and place it perfectly—the furniture in the room, the paintings on the wall, the dirty dishes in the sink—all of those elements that make the setting of your movie seem real.

Well, you're not a big Hollywood production company. So let's review a few lessons in MAKING DO, shall we? Creating the sets for your movie without a stash of cash requires brainpower and elbow grease. Be practical with your in-house resources.

If your script calls for a scene in a little girl's room . . . well, you'd better start charming your little sister so you can use her bedroom. If she says *NO WAY* take down the posters in your room and pin up some of her handmade "artwork" instead. Throw some stuffed animals on your bed, drape an old sheet over your work desk, and you're ready to shoot.

You'll get better at these transformations with experience. Turn the basement into a warehouse by filling it with empty boxes and a couple of old filing cabinets. Or convert the family room into a hipster London flat by hiding your mother's Barry Manilow records, adding your best friend's lava lamp, and hanging a few mod-looking posters. You get the idea—set design the thrift store way.

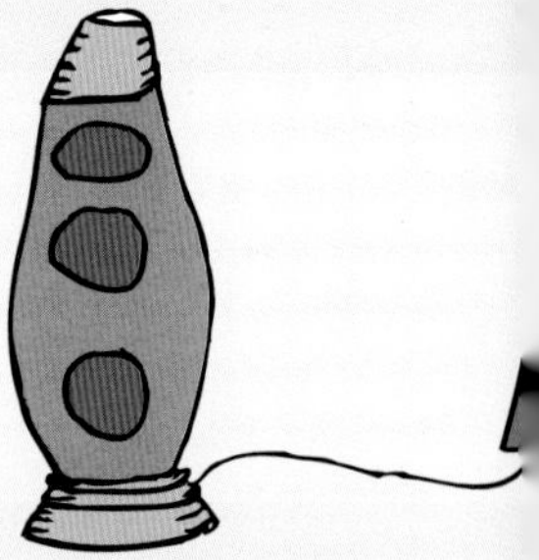

More elaborate or unusual settings will take harder work. If your story calls for a scene on the surface of the moon, and all you've got is a backyard to work with, it's time to learn how to *cheat the shot.* Set up the camera so that it frames only the small, most barren part of the yard, and drape a black sheet behind it. *(Hey, this isn't* Lawrence of Arabia. *Paint a couple of stars in the background and believe.)*

If you want a scene in a ritzy old mansion, get a few outside shots of one of those old estates in town. Then record the rest inside your small bedroom, which you've transformed, *à la Goodwill*, into a parlor. So what if you don't win any Academy Awards for set design—you've got what you need for your flick.

Prepping Your Props

Above all else, a good set designer understands the importance of the right props. Every prop on your set should reflect the time period of your flick, as well as the personality of your characters. Even the refrigerator magnets have meaning. Colorful letters of the alphabet? *Must have kids around the house.* Lots of freebee magnets from pizza delivery? *Character doesn't cook.* Those word magnets you make into poetry? *Hmm, character must have a creative side.* So pay attention to those details—you can be sure the camera will.

Make-up Please!!

Finally, we can't forget those all-important style elements: wardrobe, hair, and make-up. What are your characters wearing and what do they look like? Does it make sense for the time period and the setting? Does it tell you something about their personality? Clothes and hairstyles are visual clues to the kind of person someone is (or at least wants to be). It's also a great short-hand way to tip off your audience about the identity of a character. Think of those outrageous outfits Alicia Silverstone's character (*Cher*) wears in *Clueless*. A simple berét told you more about her in one scene than any dialogue, didn't it?

You can do the same thing for the characters in your movie. Use common sense—if a character is supposed to be a real *hep cat,* don't dress him in seersucker pants. As for hair and make-up—what would George Clooney be without the "Caesar" he sported on *ER* for all those years? His hip-yet-conservatively-short "do" said *I'm a doctor, all right, but underneath this white lab coat, I'm a temperme-ntal hottie who cares.* Or how about Meg Ryan's character in *You've Got Mail*? Her disheveled blond hair (albeit, perfectly disheveled blond hair, Hollywood-style) said *Hey, I'm as real and unpretentious as my independent bookstore and I've got more on my mind than perfect hair.* And could Adam Sandler have been half so loveable a loser in *The Wedding Singer* without those cheeseball wedding tuxedos? I don't think so. Clothes and physical appearances don't make a man or a woman—they make characters.

IMPROVISE
IMPROVISE
IMPROVISE

You can find a way to include anything in your movie if you use your imagination. Or anyone! Consider one film I helped to make: the director wanted Parker Posey (the big Hollywood actor) in a scene. Well, Parker wasn't exactly knocking down our door, so we improvised. We shot close-up shots of her from photos we ripped out of magazines. Yeah, it looks fake—but that was part of the joke in the movie. It turned out to be one of the funniest scenes.

Light as a Feather

Excerpted script, shot list, storyboard, and clips from a film by Catherine Hollander

(Thanks Catherine!)

SCRIPT

INTERIOR. NIGHT. INSIDE SEANCE ROOM/HOUSE. — 1

A boy (BILLY) is massaging the about-to-be-levitated girl's temples (AMY). The others ready for the levitation with two fingers of each hand underneath her body. She tries not to giggle. — 2

Shauna is one of those around the body. She is ayoung tomboy with greasy stringy hair and seventies clothing. She is staring in a bewildered manner. — 3

She tries to concentrate but is distracted, looking around to see if others believe what is going on. — 3, 4

The body now raises up, up over Shauna's startled face which is now in shadow. — 4

See beatific face of levitated girl. — 5

SHOT LIST

shot 1	wide of room
shot 2	med hands under body
shot 3	med of Shauna looking
shot 4	med of Shauna following face as body raises
shot 5	cu from above: face raised into light

(see p. 65 for info on framing)

STORYBOARD

1

2

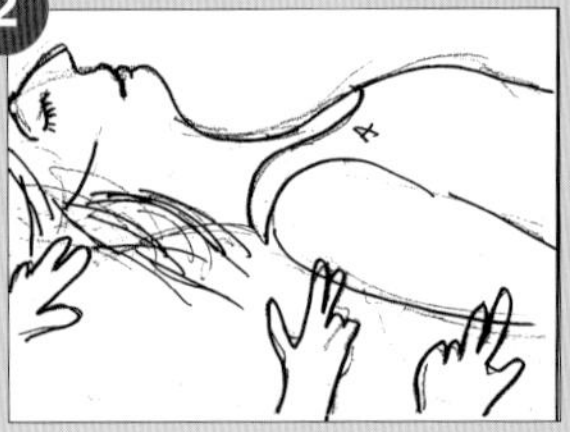

3

4

5

FILM CLIPS

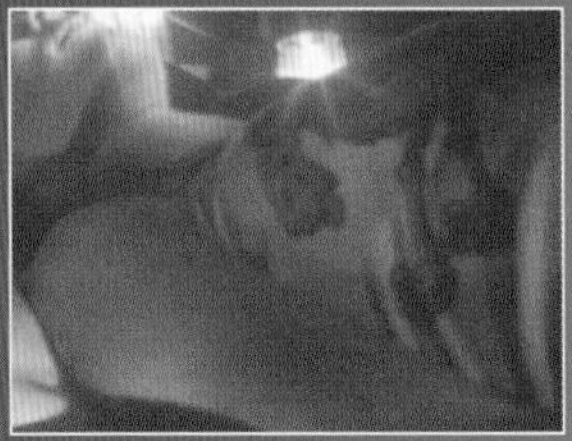

DIRECTOR'S NOTES

"This seance scene needed ghostly, moody lighting. I started with this wide, establishing shot but then made the scene mostly from medium and close-up shots—they have more emotional impact."

"In this shot, the girl lifts up and out of screen. Breaking up the action gave more sense of uncertainty and magic than showing the whole thing."

"The main actor, Isis Barker (11 years old at the time), needed to hit her lighting mark when she looked around.
It was tricky—we had lots of candles and only a few small lights.
Of course, she did it!"

"Isis ended up in shadow once the girl was 'levitated' but I liked it that way. The mystery fit the scene."

"Here, the girl's face is raised into bright light from shadow. It looks simple, but the camera and lighting crew had to build a platform in order to shoot from above."

The power of the pen?

Find out from these writers what happens when you add a movie camera to the mix.

Nora Ephron

As a screenwriter, Nora's biggest hits were When Harry Met Sally *and* Silkwood *(co-written by Alice Arlen). As a writer and director she's continued her success with* Sleepless in Seattle, Mixed Nuts, Michael, *and* You've Got Mail.

"The first movie I directed was about a woman trying to balance her career and childrearing—well, that was one of the things it was about. It seemed obvious that I should be the person to direct it. If you write scripts about women, it's hard to find directors who want to make them. So it seemed to me that I'd better become a director, if only to ensure that my scripts got made."

Jane Anderson

"Every compromise you have to make during filming can be a blessing in disguise. In 'The Baby Dance,' we found a trailer park that seemed like the perfect location. But our budget couldn't accommodate it. I had to give it up. I was starting to panic. But then we found an abandoned bunch of shacks next to a farm. My production designer brought in some trailers. We created this utterly unique world which was far more interesting. In fact, this scene was one of the stand-outs of the movie."

Jane directing Vanessa Redgrave in If These Walls Could Talk, 2. *Since Jane was a screenwriter transitioning into a director, she had a few tricks up her sleeve:*

"I'm a short girl, so I often climb up on a ladder to give my directions. It forces those who doubt my skills to look up to me."

Jane wrote and directed the first segment of HBO's If These Walls Could Talk *and* The Baby Dance. *She won an Emmy for HBO's* The Positively True Adventures of the Alleged Texas Cheerleader-Murdering Mom. *She has received numerous Emmy nominations for her writing and directing, and is an award-winning playwright as well. Her screenplays include* How to Make an American Quilt *and* It Could Happen to You.

Catherine Hollander

Catherine let us in on her moviemaking process by sharing all sorts of stuff from the shoot of her film Light as a Feather. *The short film has screened at many festivals. Catherine's made many other films and video projects and is currently at work on her next movie.*

Chapter Six

Putting It in the Can

Claudia Weill

"It's not a part-time job, it's not a full-time job, it's an obsession."

Claudia Weill

Claudia started making movies when she was a college student. Since then she's made experimental and documentary shorts, as well as the feature films Girlfriends, The Other Half of the Sky, *and* It's My Turn. *If you haven't caught her work on the big screen (and you should) you may have seen one of the many episodes she's directed for TV shows like* My So-Called Life, Sesame Street, *and* Chicago Hope.

Finally. Here's the moment you've been waiting for—turning that camera on, and hitting that *Record* button (or if you're using a Super 8, pushing that trigger). All of this time planning the shoot—now you get to shoot the plan!

It's no coincidence that many film and video directors are also painters or photographers. Famous directors and filmmakers like Lizzie Borden, Joan Chen, and Amy Heckerling all started out as different kinds of visual artists. It makes sense! Moviemaking is all about composition, color, and framing—just like other art forms. So if people say you've "got a good eye," now's the time to use it. (And if people *haven't* said that, they will after they see your first flick.)

One note before you read on: the following examples are just that—*examples.* There is no right way to make your movie, so don't feel restricted to these ideas. Go with your instincts and experiment with different techniques to see which work best for you. After all, you're the one calling the shots.

How to Make Your Own Brilliant Career:

A Mini-Interview with Gillian Armstrong

How did you get started?

"I wanted to do something with my love of theater, art, and literature. I studied production design at art school and then decided to major in film. I became an editor first, then a director."

What are the most important qualities for a director to have?

"Passion, dedication, and vision. A love of the visual arts, actors, and storytelling. Plus the ability to work with a team. Do it because you have something you want to say, not for glamour or fame."

What's the best part?

"Being on the set for a brilliant moment of performance and knowing you've got it on film!"

Advice for Girl Directors?

"Watch great movies. Learn still photography. Start using your eyes. Just do it—make something no matter how small. Doing is learning."

Gillian Armstrong

Gillian on the set of Little Women.

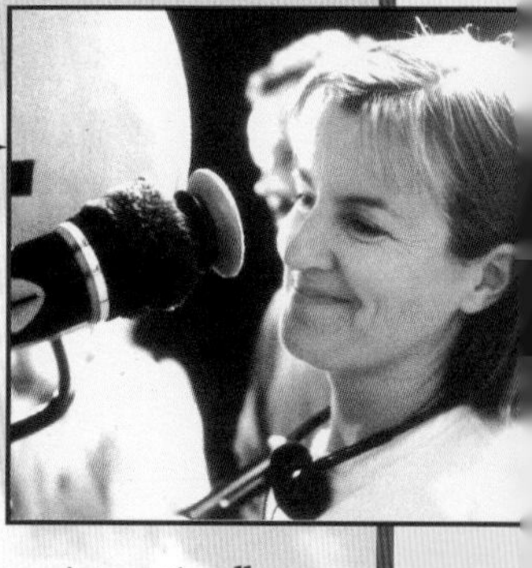

In 1979 Gillian blazed the trail for Aussie women directors with the debut of her first film, My Brilliant Career. *Since then she's become an internationally acclaimed director for a long list of movies:* Starstruck, Mrs. Soffel, High Tide, The Last Days of Chez Nous, Little Women, Oscar & Lucinda, *and* Charlotte Gray.

Start with the Simple Stuff

Let's review your basic checklist, shall we?

☑ Clean the camera lens.

Pull out your handy *camera care kit* (You DID make one, right?) and clean the lens with canned air, lens tissues, or that soft T-shirt you've outgrown. (Remember: don't rub, gently wipe the lens.)

☑ Charge the batteries.

And always have an extra fully-charged one on the set. There is nothing like driving deep into the woods only to realize that you left the extra battery in your bedroom. Losing power halfway through your shoot *stinks*.

☑ Load the film or videotape.

Tapes and Super 8 cartridges fit easily into the camera compartment, and the chamber lid should close easily. Don't force it—you might break your camera. If there is a problem, make sure the compartment is free of dust and gunk. If you *still* can't get it into position, go see the pros at your nearest camera shop.

☑ Take off the lens cap.

Duh. You'd never make this mistake—right? Well, you'd be surprised at what can happen in the rush of setting up your shots. I've been there before—looking into the viewfinder, seeing only black and PANICKING. (*My camera's busted!*) It happens to everyone. At least I hope so.

☑ Turn on the camera.

Woohoo! Just when you thought we'd never get there.

☑ Open your eyes!

Go ahead and shoot with *both* eyes open. Using both eyes allows you to see the action through the viewfinder AND the action around you. That way you won't step off a 40-foot cliff recording that gorgeous waterfall. It takes a little practice, but you'll get the hang of it.

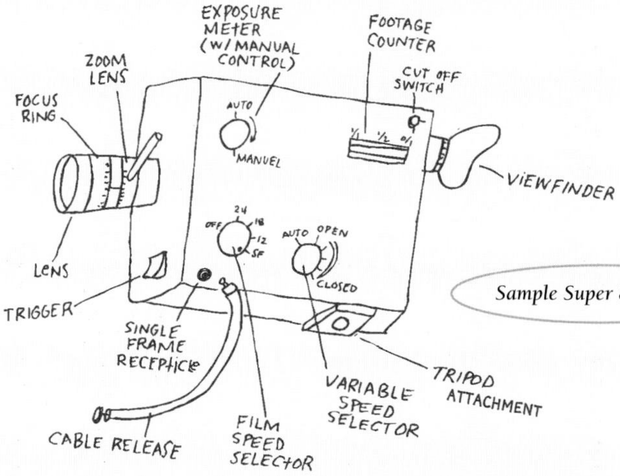

Sample Super 8 camera

Set Up Your Shots

When you compose your shot, you should carefully choose each element that will appear in the frame. Because everything you see through the viewfinder WILL show up on screen. So there you'll be, at the big premiere of your movie and the first thing you'll notice is that horrible bowl of artificial fruit your mom keeps on the coffee table. Or the "Drink Milk" ad on the bus stop behind your actors. *How did that get there?* you'll ask yourself. I *didn't even notice that when I shot that scene*. Too late—now it's Rosie O'Donnell (with a fake milk mustache) who's stealing the show, and not your lead character.

To avoid this catastrophe, pay close attention to the composition of your shots *before you shoot them*. That means spending time "dressing" your shots—getting rid of the stuff you don't want to see and taking the time (it only takes a few minutes!) to arrange your shots perfectly.

Learn to Frame

Su Friedrich

"I think the most important thing is to learn how to see. You can have the best camera, the best lights, and the best tripod in the world, but if you don't know how to compose an image, or have a sense internally of how you want things to look, then it's all going to be a waste of time and money."

Su Friedrich

Composing a shot means learning to frame it in a very deliberate, careful way. Even if you're filming a fire-eating, snake-handling actor while you swing on a trapeze, take the time to frame your shot!

As an exercise, look through your camera viewfinder now. Concentrate on seeing *everything* that's in your frame. Think of it as a blank canvas, or an ordinary picture frame. What would you like to see there?

Compose Like a Pro

Don't cut off your actors' heads (or any other body parts, for that matter), unless you're making a horror flick. In general, people look funny without feet or the tops of their heads, so take care to compose your shot so that it includes all important limbs.

Vary your camera's viewpoint. Don't shoot every scene in your movie from the same camera position. That would be *borr-ing*. Your movie will look better and give a better sense of space if you switch camera angles and change perspectives. (Don't worry, I'll give you plenty of tips on camera perspectives on the next page.)

Follow the "Rule of Thirds." Instead of placing your main actors or events directly in the middle of the frame, place them slightly *off center*. It helps to imagine your frame being divided into thirds—then you can organize the key elements of your shot along these imaginary lines. That's the *rule of thirds*—it's a more interesting way to organize your shot composition than just sticking the important stuff right smack in the middle of the frame.

Take a good look at the background of your shot. Funny things can happen on film or video. You didn't even *notice* that plant on the bookshelf behind your actor, but when you review your footage, it looks like she has leaves sprouting out of her ears. *Drats*. Get rid of those unwanted attention-grabbers in the background.

Su with her Mom on the set of The Ties that Bind, *an experimental documentary about her mother.*

Su's made 13 award winning films, including Hide and Seek, Sink or Swim, *and* The Ties that Bind. *From start to finish, Su does every aspect of movie production herself—from shooting the film to editing the final picture.*

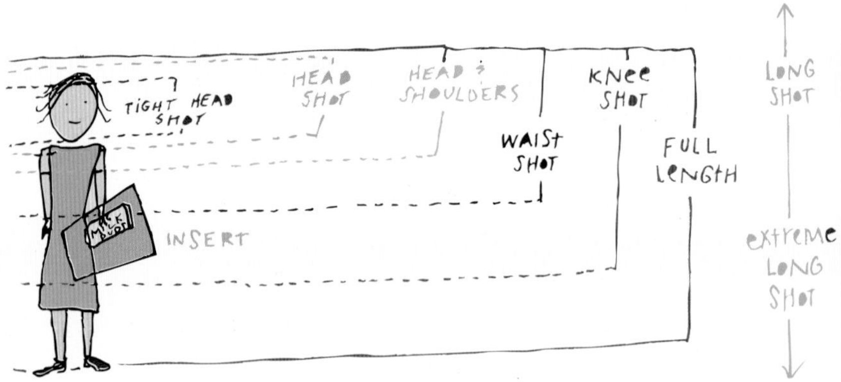

Long shot
(LS)

Medium shot
(MS)

The Long and the Short of Framing—

There are three basic types of frames, and many variations on all three:

The long shot (LS) (also called a wide shot)
In a long shot, the camera's frame includes your main subject, in entirety, plus the surroundings. (If it's an actor, for example, it's ALL of her.) The camera appears to be far away from the subject.

The medium shot (MS):
Your frame includes much of the object or person you're filming and little else. A medium shot might be of a person from the waist up.

The close-up (CU):
Every actor's dream shot—the frame could include all of an actor's face, for example. Or if it's extremely concentrated, even just one part of the person's face. The key is that a close-up reveals *detail*.

Close-up
(CU)

Keep in mind you will almost never get the perfect shot the first time—an actor messes up a line, your cat runs into the frame, a light you rigged to the ceiling hits you on the head. What do you do? You shoot it again, which is making another *take*. That's why, on movie sets, people are always saying "Take 2" or "Take 22!" or (on a really long day) "Take 222!" They are shooting multiple takes of the same shot.

For time's sake, you shouldn't bother making a million (or even more than a few) takes of a single shot. You want to get this movie made soon, right? Additional takes use up time and money. So let the perfectionist in you take a coffee break—get it as right as you can in a few takes and move on!

As you shoot your movie, keep track of all the takes you make by writing them down in a *shot log*. (If you have an AD or a DP on set—that's *her* job!) That way you'll have a written description of each take and shot.

Clear the way for your long shot!

When filming a long shot, make sure you notice everything in the frame. That's because objects in the far background have a sneaky way of ending up in your shot. For example, it's impossible for me to pull off a long shot in my apartment because of, well, the junk everywhere. That dirty laundry in the corner, or the old camera equipment on the floor would always end up in the shot.

Jocelyn Moorhouse

"Never be intimidated by the technical experts and don't be afraid to ask dumb questions like: 'Should that electrician be reflected in that mirror?' Often no one notices these things except you. Because as Director you notice EVERYTHING."

JOCELYN MOORHOUSE

Award-winning films directed by Jocelyn Moorhouse include Proof *(which she also wrote),* How to Make An American Quilt, *and* A Thousand Acres. *A native of Melbourne, she developed her short film* The Siege of Barton's Bathroom *into a series for Australian TV. Joceyln also co-produced the movies* Muriel's Wedding *and* Unconditional Love.

Moving the Camera: Steady as She Goes

Yvonne Rainer

YVONNE RAINER
on the most essential quality for a director:

"Drive!"

***Yvonne is one of the most renowned avant-garde film-makers around. Her films include* Film About a Woman Who . . ., Kristina Talking Pictures, Journeys from Berlin/1971, *and* Privilege.**

Shots can be static or moving. When the camera moves in any way during a shot, it's called a *moving shot.* If the camera stays in one stationary position, it's *static*. This is true even if there is lots of moving action in front of the camera—your actors could be doing cart-wheels, but if the camera stays in one place, it's a static shot.

You can do a STATIC SHOT one of two ways:

Hand-Held

A *hand-held* shot is exactly what it sounds like. Hold on to the camera and try to stand still, like a statue. Remember, even your breath is going to be detected by the camera as movement, so hold it as long as you can without turning blue in the face. Hand-held stationary shots are easier if you find something stable you can rest the bottom of the camera on, such as a table. It also helps to have something to lean on—like a wall or a good friend—for better balance.

Tripod

If you've got one, a tripod is a beautiful thing—mostly because it will allow you to film and breathe at the same time. The camera attaches to the head of the tripod, which keeps the camera absolutely still.

To make a MOVING SHOT with a hand-held camera:

1. Get a good grip on the camera. Even light-weight cameras get heavy after a while, so find a comfy way to hold on while keeping your fingers free to operate the controls. If you're right-handed, grip the camera with your right hand and place your left hand under the camera's body for additional support. And if you're a lefty, do it the opposite way.
2. With your arms bent, rest your elbows against your body for rigid support. Try to keep the camera steady and avoid jerky movements.
3. Rehearse the movement you'll be using before you press *Record* or start to film. That way you'll know if you can keep your balance.
4. Don't move too fast. Try to use a consistent speed throughout the movement and slow to a gentle stop. Moving your camera too quickly makes shots blurry and unwatch-able.

Sure, this all sounds easy, but learning how to manage and move your camera without making your audience seasick takes some practice. Slow and steady is always best!

Get into the Groove and MOVE!

You're not the type of gal who likes to stand still, right? To get where the action is you've got to move around.

Pan and Tilt

No, it's not an amusement park ride. *Pan* and *tilt* are the two camera movements you'll probably use most often. They're both simple:

Panning

How would you capture the action on a tennis court? By following the ball back and forth. The motion you're making with your head as you follow the tennis ball is a *pan*.

When you pan the camera, you simply move the camera horizontally along a straight line, from left to right, or vice-versa.

Using a tripod makes panning really smooth and easy. But it's not always possible to use a tripod so it's good to know how to execute a hand-held pan, too.

A super-fast pan, in which the camera moves very quickly and blurs motion, is called a whip pan.

How to make your HAND-HELD PAN as smooth as silk:

1. Hold the camera as steady as you can.
2. Gracefully follow the subject or action you are recording (a tennis ball, for example) by slowly moving your camera horizontally.
3. When you reach the end point of the action, pause for a few seconds, then stop recording.

Tilting

Tilting is the same thing as *panning*, except that it's a vertical movement (up and down). *A warning for those big tilt shots:* Don't tilt so far up that you fall over backwards. You could hurt your camera, not to mention yourself.

Tracking

A tracking shot is made by moving along with the subject at roughly the same pace. If the shot involves moving a long distance, you'll want to come up with something creative to use for transportation (i.e., a dolly that can carry you). Some of my favorite make-shift dollies are: a grocery cart (enlist a friend to push), a skateboard, or if you know somebody who can drive, a car.

Crane

A crane shot is a lot like tracking, except you move the camera in a *rise and fall* movement along with your subject. Say someone is climbing a tree—if you want to record them with a crane shot you'll start by kneeling down while your subject is on the ground. Then as they climb the tree, slowly rise by gradually straightening your legs. That way the camera will follow them up the tree. Easy!

Make local, Think global

Dang-blast it! Because this book is only so long, there are lots of amazing women directors who don't get mentioned in these pages. Female filmmakers are making movies all over the world, so don't forget to check the foreign film section at your local video store. (And please, don't be a sissy about subtitles.) Here are just a few women directors whose movies will make you glad you did:

Gilda de Abreu (Brazil)
Rakhshan Bani Etemad (Iran)
María Luisa Bemberg (Argentina)
Liliana Cavani (Italy)
Vêra Chytilová (Czech Republic)
Claire Denis (France)
Judit Elek (Hungary)
Safi Faye (Senegal)
Marcela Fernández Violante (Mexico)
Sara Gómez (Cuba)
Marion Hänsel (France)
Angieska Holland (Poland)
Ann Hui (Hong Kong)
Beeban Kidron (England)
Diane Kurys (France)
Matilde Soto Landeta (Mexico)
Sarah Maldoror (France)
Marilú Mallet (Chile)
Márta Mészáros (Hungary)
Pilar Miró (Spain)
Kira Muratova (Ukraine)
Mira Nair (India/United States)
Euzhan Palcy (France)
Sally Potter (England)
Helma Sanders-Brahms (Germany)
Kinuyo Tanaka (Japan)
Monika Treut (Germany)
Liv Ullmann (Sweden)
Agnès Varda (France)
Lina Wertmüller (Italy)

Cruising for a Cool Shot

Amazing shots can be taken from a moving car. Just roll down the window and direct your driver to the perfect speed. If you're using a video camera, watch out for wind sounds on the microphone—it's best to keep the camcorder inside the car. But if you're using a Super 8 camera, you can hang that camera way out the window, since it doesn't pick up sound. (Be sure to hang on and watch out for oncoming cars! Remember those horror stories from grade school about kids' arms getting lopped off? You want to hang on to your camera AND your arm.)

You'll get great landscape scenes from these kinds of traveling shots. Use this technique in city streets too, and don't feel limited to using cars. Motorcycles, subways, trains, scooters, skateboards—any form of transportation—can make for a fantastic tracking shot.

Get an Angle on the Action

Finding the perfect angle on the action requires some craftiness. Should you find yourself climbing a fire escape or scrambling through city sewers, rest assured that's the mark of a determined artist. If you're filming on location (on a busy street or in a crowded shopping center), this can be especially challenging.

First of all, move around to see where you can place (or hold) the camera to get the most dynamic perspective. You may want to shoot directly at *eye-level* to the action, or from *above* or *below* your subjects.

You can use different camera angles to convey moods, or even psychological states. For instance, recording from a *high angle* suggests that the camera has a domineering presence over the action, whereas an *eye-level* shot suggests that the camera (and the filmmakers) are more objective. Shooting scenes from a *low angle* camera position makes your subjects look larger than life—buildings loom like skyscrapers and people look more powerful.

Another cool camera perspective is the *point of view* shot—when you're recording the *point of view* of the main character. In this kind of shot, the camera is essentially acting as the character's eyes. Say the action is a bank robber looking down to discover that the stash of cash in her bag has disappeared. You might want to show the empty bag as she sees it, from her perspective. That means excluding her head and shoulders from the frame and focusing attention on the object she's looking at—the vast emptiness of her bag.

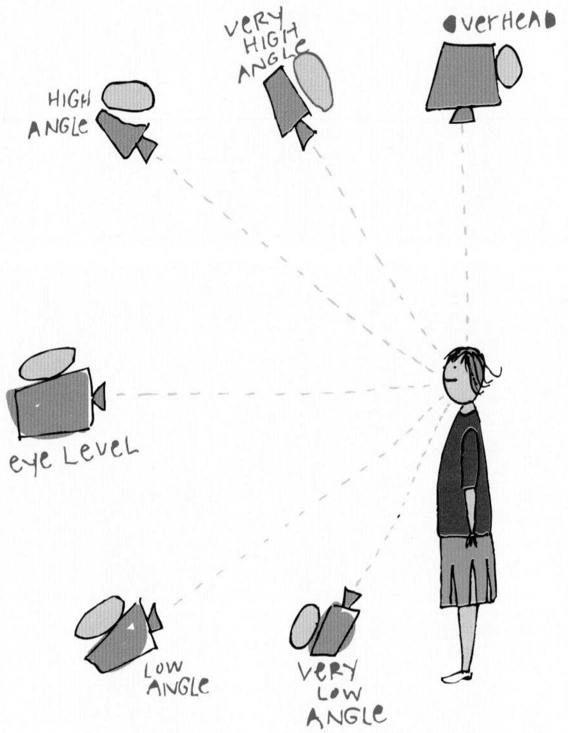

Sample camera angles

Over the shoulder

Actor's point of view

LOW ANGLES

In many music videos, you'll notice that band performances are often filmed from low angles, which makes the viewer feel like they are right there watching the band perform on stage.

That Zany Little Thing Called ZOOM

The camera angles that we've covered so far: *low, high, eye-level,* and *point-of-view*—all come from the positioning of your camera. To get the one you want, you must physically move your camera. But there are other ways to capture movement and different perspectives, and they're built right into your camera.

The most important of these features is the ZOOM lens. The zoom lens changes the size of the frame perspective by moving *toward* (zooming in) or *away from* (zooming out) your subject. With the click of a button (or turn of a zoom handle), you can vary the size of your shot without moving your camera.

The easiest way to understand your zoom is to mess around with it!

CAUTION: Only use the zoom if you can't get close enough to your subject, AND, if you have a steady tripod. Because when you zoom, every little jitter of your camera is recorded. Also, repeated use of your zoom lens will make your audience sick. Don't fall prey to zoom overkill.

Confused about camera movements or shot perspectives?

Need help with cinematography?

Want to share production notes with other emerging film and video makers?

Go to Cyber Film School! You'll find it at *www.cyberfilmschool.com*

This enormous Web site offers all sorts of great information on moviemaking, and tons of links to other sites. You'll find answers to all of your questions about motion picture and video production.

Cyberfilmschool.com will lead you to—

The Internet Filmmaker's FAQ . . . . *www.filmmaking.net*

Film Underground . . . . *www.filmunderground.com*

Guerrilla Filmmaking 101 . . . . *www.angelfire.com/biz/proletariatpictures/r101.html*

Reelends.com . . . . *www.reelends.com*

And my personal favorite for all general help!

Exposure: The Internet Resource for Young Filmmakers . . . *www.exposure.co.uk*

Susan Seidelman

Desperately Seeking Advice?

"Be confident about what you know, but not afraid to admit what you don't. You have to be smart enough to use the best ideas—and sometimes someone else on your crew will have a better idea than you do. Part of the skill of being a good director is to recognize the best idea, no matter who it comes from."

SUSAN SEIDELMAN

Susan's award winning movies, like Smithereens, Desperately Seeking Susan, *and* She-Devil *are filled with funky, independently minded heroines. (You'll surely recognize the actor who stars as one of these characters—Madonna played the lead role in* Desperately Seeking Susan *before she was famous). Susan's also directed episodes of HBO's show* Sex in the City, *and other feature films including,* The Making of Mr. Right, Confessions of a Suburban Girl, *and* Gaudi Afternoon.

Hit 'Em with Your Best Shot

Composing your shot, unfortunately, is only half the battle of getting a good take. After all, it doesn't matter if you take an hour to frame the right shot if the lighting is bad. Or if your camera's out of focus. Or if the sound is garbled . . . well, you get the idea. There are plenty of other problems to worry about. The next section will help you remember them.

1. Keep Your Focus!

Most camcorders, and some Super 8 cameras, have an automatic focus to keep your subjects sharp. These are sophisticated electronic systems that control the lens. Most of the time, auto-focus will work just fine for your moviemaking. Your camera will interpret what the lens sees and keep it in focus, even when the subject or the camera is moving. But auto-focus isn't foolproof. It's your job to keep the focus when your camera can't.

Setting your focus manually isn't difficult: First, you'll want to switch the camera to manual focus. (There should be a button or switch on your camera—check your camera's manual if you can't find it.) Next, find the *focus ring* on the lens barrel of your camera. Use a free finger to rotate it while you look through the viewfinder. The blurry subjects you see will grow sharp as you rotate the focus ring. When everything in frame is sharp, you've got the camera in focus.

Here's the easiest technique: Before you film or record a shot, zoom all the way in on your subject, focus the lens, and then zoom out to where you want your shot to be. If your subject moves, you'll need to keep adjusting your focus to compensate for their motion. Manual focus does take some practice, so don't expect perfect results the first few times you try it.

Hey Lady, Learn Your Lenses!

"Whenever anybody says, 'Hey, I wanna direct, what can I do?' My advice? Take an acting class and get yourself a 35mm still camera with interchangeable lenses and shoot everything—then write down what lens you use. This way you'll learn what different lenses do."

Melanie Mayron
(see p. 74 for more on Melanie)

Melanie Mayron knows her lenses, do you?

You'll probably want to use manual focus when you are . . .

. . . ***Shooting fast moving subjects.***
If you follow a subject which is moving quickly through the frame, auto-focus may get confused about where to focus.

. . . ***Shooting in low-light situations.***
Auto-focus is less trustworthy in low-light situations, or when you're shooting dark subjects. If your shot involves either, use manual focus to be sure. (Two General Tips: #1 Avoid dark backgrounds. #2 Tell your actors not to wear black or red clothing.)

. . . ***Shooting through a screen door, fence, or any other type of partition.***
Auto-focus will focus on anything that is immediately in front of the camera—the fence, for example, rather than the activity *beyond* the fence. Switch to manual focus to ensure that your focus is where you want it to be.

2. Sound Check

Checking your sound is critical. Every time you hit *Record*, you're recording sound as well as pictures. Sound makes up your movie as much as pictures do. So pay attention to what you hear by performing a "sound check" first.

Here's how: The camcorder should have a socket where you can plug in headphones—headphones off any old Walkman will do. Put them on, and you should be able to hear exactly what the built in microphone is picking up. With the camera recording, notice the *ambient sounds* that you hear—the noise that remains after you tell everyone on the set to be quiet. Background noises can obscure your actors' lines and confuse your audience—noises like airplanes flying overhead or dogs barking in the distance. If you hear noises like that during your check, wait to record until they've stopped. (Or move to a quieter location.)

While you're doing your sound check, ask your actors to rehearse some of their lines. That way you can tell ahead of time if they are audible—if not, ask them to speak up!

Watch the Wind

When you're using a video camcorder outside, shield the microphone from wind noise by standing behind something. You can also turn your back to the wind to buffer the blows. Even a breeze can rattle the microphone and affect sound quality.

Mic Test

Test your camcorder's sound range by asking a friend to read from a book while you record her. As you record, move slowly away and find the maximum distance at which you can still hear the words clearly. Note that distance, and take care not to move beyond it when you begin recording for real.

3. Get Good Exposures!

Recording just the right image—with all the right colors, shadows, and details—is all about getting the right *exposure*. And getting the right exposure is all about getting the right amount of light.

The good news is that most cameras (video, DV, or Super 8) do this for you. They are set to give you *normal exposure* with a system that adjusts to available light automatically. (Normal exposure means as close as possible to what we see with our eyes.) Many camcorders have such sophisticated exposure systems that you can record in very low light, or even at night.

SUPER COOL!

If you're using a camcorder or digital video camera, special features (like focus and sound) will be fully automated, so don't sweat it too much. BUT, you can start by switching the automatic controls off—that way you'll learn to do it yourself.

"Reshooting a scene is not a sign of weakness."

Nora Ephron

(see p. 61 for more on Nora)

Look Out for the Light!

So how do you know how much light you need?

Moviemaking is often called "painting with light," and this is where you learn how to control your palette.

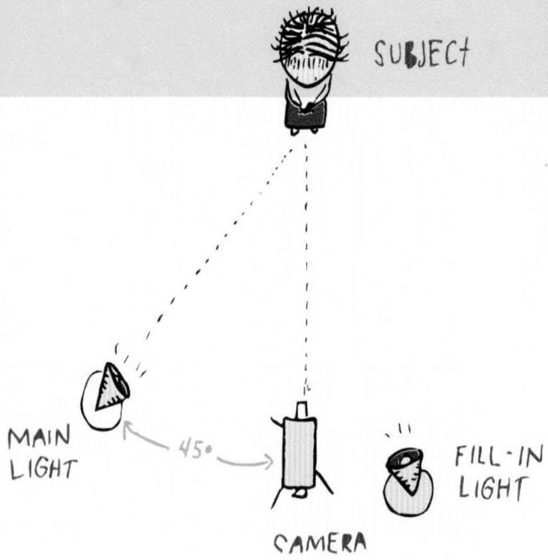

Overhead view of two-light arrangement

Turn It On, Girl

If you're shooting indoors you may want to "give a boost" to the natural light. Turn on every available light in the room and survey what you've got. Need more light? Take off lamp-shades to increase the room's overall light level. You can also replace lightbulbs with higher watt bulbs, or bring in lamps from other rooms. Try opening doors to allow light to spill in from other areas. If the room is particularly dark, you may want to make a trip to the hardware store to buy cheap, clip-on lamps—the kind usually used in car garages. Just make sure you keep these lights *off* camera—outside of your camera's picture frame. You want the light, but you don't want your audience to see where it's coming from.

Another way to increase your light is to use *reflectors*, which can bounce light directly onto your set. You can make a reflector out of a piece of cardboard covered with aluminum foil, or you can use the sun shades people stick in their car windows. Use your reflector to redirect light from a lamp by positioning it at a good *bounce* angle—so that it "bounces" light onto your set. This sort of lighting is usually softer than direct light, so it creates an image that is less stark.

Watch Your Back

Backlighting is bad news. Period. That's when the main source of light comes from *behind* a subject and shines directly into the camera. Avoid placing your actors or subjects in front of a bright window, because the camera will automatically adjust to the light behind them (the *backlight*) and leave your actor as a silhouette. If you want your actor to walk in front of a window, move your camera to the side to keep the window out of the background. Backlighting can also be a problem outside if you've positioned your subject in front of the sun. See, your camera's aimed directly at that big source of light. Keep the sun BEHIND your camera and you'll get a better image.

As you should know by now, lighting is just as much an art as writing, shooting, and editing. There are plenty of good books, manuals, and Web sites with more information on creative lighting techniques. But as always, the best way to learn is by doing it yourself. Start experimenting!

"Understand light. This is an important thing and takes a bit of learning. To learn about how light reacts, go out and make tests with your camera. Take notes and watch what you've shot."

KATE HAUG

(see p. 94 for a pic of Kate touring with the Super Super 8 festival)

Underexposure is what happens when your film or video doesn't get enough light. When played back or projected, an underexposed movie yields a picture that is too dark—you can't see details and the color looks muddy. **Worst-case scenario: a black screen.**

Overexposure occurs when you film or record in *too much* light. It can make the picture seem washed out. **Worst case scenario: a white screen.**

Calling for Action from Your Actors

Everything on your set is ready to roll. You've got the camera and lighting figured out, and your script in hand. But now comes the tricky part: directing your actors. This is where you really get to show your skills as field general, diplomat, and psychologist—all at the same time.

Chances are you won't be working with professional actors, but with some willing friends and family members. So it may be your first time making a movie, but it's their first time too! Remember that.

The relationship between you and your actors is critical to their performance. Good morale on set makes for a good movie. You want to be friendly and flexible, and you want your cast to have fun . . . but you also want to get your work done. You *can* do both.

Let's assume that you gave your actors copies of the script long before the shoot. (You did, *right*?) They should know their lines and actions for each scene. But before rolling camera, discuss the particular shot or scene with them again and choreograph their movement within the frame. Don't tell them exactly how to say a line, but talk with them about their character's motivation, personality, and purpose in the story. If there's more than one person in the shot, be sure you tell them where they should be looking, who they are speaking to, and what they are doing with the rest of their body. Stage a rehearsal, so you can clear up any confusion. Above all, be supportive of your actors' needs. It's hard to get in front of a camera, let alone *act*.

Gurinder Chadha

"If you had never been to Los Angeles or America and were from Britain (like me), you would have no idea of the Latino and Asian influence in California. I was shocked when I first came to L.A. I would look around and see Latinos on the street and think they were Indian. You'd have no idea about that diversity if you were living in Europe. So what we did with 'What's Cooking' was try and show that kind of America. The one that's really out there, but that audiences never get to see on the screen. I wanted to take what I see happening around me culturally and celebrate it."

Gurinder Chadha

*Gurinder began her directing career with several award-winning documentaries—*I'm British But *and* Acting Our Age, *are just a few. She then directed her first feature film, the incredible* Bhaji on the Beach. What's Cooking, *her most recent film, stars another woman who does great work behind the camera too—Joan Chen.*

Gurinder directing her cast and crew on the set of What's Cooking.

Break the Molds

Statistics say that 70% of girls want to look, dress, or fix their hair like characters they see on TV. Okay, so if you watch the same TV shows I do, that means everybody wants to look like some white, skinny chick with long blonde hair. Pretty limited, wouldn't you say? As we all know, the world is not filled with gals who look like clones from *Baywatch*. Take it upon yourself, Girl Director, to do your part for the 99.9% of us who aren't Pamela Anderson and cast people who don't fit the Hollywood mold.

Diversify!

On-the-Street Etiquette

Unless you plan on filming in your home all the time, you'll need to learn some moviemaking etiquette for the street. People respond strangely to someone with a camera—some folks like to ham it up and get in your face, while others feel uncomfortable. When your set is the street, you're in the public eye and everyone notices the person with the camera. That's especially true when she's running down the street chasing a shot, or climbing a street light to get a better angle. You'll find yourself talking to a lot of people about what you're doing, so get comfortable chatting it up.

In general, respect the privacy of other people. Don't record people you don't know unless they are in large crowds or you've gotten their permission beforehand.

On that note, anyone who appears in your movie should sign a release form, which grants you their permission to use their image or voice. Release forms keep you legit and prevent all sorts of legal binds. For instance, say your lead actor decides she doesn't want to be in your flick anymore, *after* you've shot and edited the whole movie. That's a major bummer *unless* you've got that release form from her. (*Special note: Release forms for actors under 18 must also be signed by their parent or legal guardian.*)

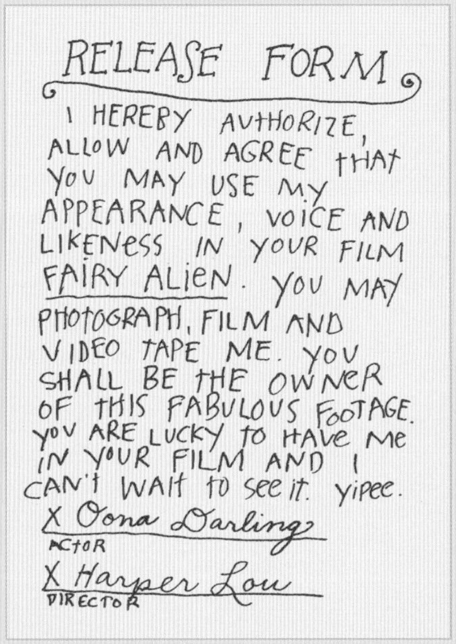

RELEASE FORM

I HEREBY AUTHORIZE, ALLOW AND AGREE THAT YOU MAY USE MY APPEARANCE, VOICE AND LIKENESS IN YOUR FILM FAIRY ALIEN. YOU MAY PHOTOGRAPH, FILM AND VIDEO TAPE ME. YOU SHALL BE THE OWNER OF THIS FABULOUS FOOTAGE. YOU ARE LUCKY TO HAVE ME IN YOUR FILM AND I CAN'T WAIT TO SEE IT. YIPEE.

X Oona Darling
ACTOR

X Harper Lou
DIRECTOR

Gillian Anderson

"I suddenly realized that I had something to say—I'd been having creative visions for some time that had to do with me controlling shots rather than being controlled."

GILLIAN ANDERSON

Gillian Anderson, the star of the hit series The X-Files, *debuted as a director by taking over the set for one episode. Gillian wrote and directed the episode, and "found it ESSENTIAL to know beat by beat what I was going to shoot before I showed up on set." Look for her to move on to feature films someday. Until then, her advice on directing is to "RIDE THE FEAR AND DO IT."*

Melanie Mayron

Melanie on the set of The Baby-Sitters Club.

"As a director, you get to control it all. You bring the story to the screen. So find a story that you're really passionate about—love the material because you're going to be working on it for a while. When I did 'The Baby-Sitters Club,' I realized that as the director, I was the only one there from start to finish. So I better really love it."

Melanie has played many meaty roles—a hitchhiker in Harry and Tonto, *a prostitute in* Hustling, *and an independent photographer in* Girlfriends *(directed by Claudia Weill, remember?). She also starred in the television series* thirtysomething. *Well, today you can find her on both sides of the camera. She directed the feature film* The Baby-Sitters Club *and the TV movies* Toothless, *and a remake of* Freaky Friday.

Ready, Set, Rolling

You've heard the phrase "lights, camera, action!" That's not exactly how it goes on a big set. Here's the basic "call routine" to get the cameras rolling:

Quiet on the set!

1. The AD (Assistant Director) calls "Quiet on the set!" which is a professional way of telling people to SHUT UP so there won't be any interference.

Ready!

2. Director signals cast and crew to get ready by saying "Ready." *Clever, huh?*

Sound!

3. AD or Director calls "Sound!" signaling the Soundperson to start recording.

Speed!

4. Soundperson (or Director) responds by turning on sound, doing a sound check and saying "Speed!" when she's recording.

Camera!

5. The AD or Director yells "Camera" telling the camera person to start filming.

Mark!

6. The clapper comes in front of the camera to mark the shot.

Action!

7. *The moment you've been waiting for.* The Director (that's you!) yells "Action!," telling the actors to start the scene. You'll roll camera until you've got what you want, then yell "Cut!"

There you have it! That's how the shots are called on most productions. You can follow it to the "T," or make up your own version—use what works best for you and your crew. Or if your crew is just me, myself, and I—talk to yourself. (At least someone is listening.)

Look Familiar?

Yeah, you may already know these women directors as actors on hit TV shows.

Well guess what they do on the other side of the camera.

"Filmmaking is a collaborative art, but it does need one person to say YES, NO. Right here. Roll camera. But as the director you also have to be able to say, 'that's stupid, forget what I just said.' After the lights are all set up. 'Let's change everything, I made a mistake.' "

Betty Thomas

"When you're an actor you have to have a very high level of energy and then totally cut off and relax. But a director has to be very high all the time. All day long—there's no such thing as down time."

BETTY THOMAS

Betty won her way into our homes as Lucy Bates on **Hill Street Blues.** *She segued from being on TV, to operating the controls behind it, directing episodes of the TV shows* **Hooperman, Doogie Howser,** *and* **Dream On.** *After winning Emmy Awards for her work on both sides of the camera, she's gone on to direct numerous feature films, including* **The Brady Bunch Movie, The Late Shift, Private Parts, Dr. Dolittle,** *and* **28 Days.**

Chapter Seven

Finish That Flick!

"When I applied to film school they told me I couldn't be a director because I was a woman. **They were wrong.**"

MARTHA COOLIDGE

Martha Coolidge

Thank goodness Martha didn't listen to the naysayers who thought a girl didn't belong behind the camera. Martha not only made it through film school, but also has gone on to become one of the most successful directors in Hollywood. Of the many TV shows and movies she's directed, here are just a few of her feature films: Valley Girl, Rambling Rose, Out to Sea, *and* Introducing Dorothy Dandridge.

YOU DID IT! YOU DID IT! YOU DID IT!

You shot your movie! After the frantic pace of production—the 9 A.M. calls (*Krispy Kremes!*), the occasional artistic "disagreement" (*All made up now!*), and that one set you rebuilt out of chicken wire (*Fast thinking!*)—here you sit. It's quiet now, and all you've got in front of you are a few little tapes or film cartridges. Congratulate yourself on a job well done, but don't get too comfy. The fact is you're just halfway to the finish line. Now's the time for the post-production push!

Post-production is the final stage in which you put it all together: you'll review and edit your footage, add sound or visual effects, and maybe even some music. Basically, think of the shots you've gotten "in the can" as pieces of a puzzle—post-production is where you'll assemble all those pieces into one brilliant whole.

The size of your post-production job depends on a number of factors, including: how you've shot your footage, the format of your camera, and the editing equipment you'll be using. There are countless ways to tackle the rest of the process. It's your job to figure out which one works best for you.

Illustration: Old-school-style linear editing machine

Developing the Film

If you've shot your movie on Super 8 film, your first step will be sending the exposed cartridges to a lab for processing. (See the Resource Guide in the back of the book for film developers.) This step is as easy as writing down an address and dropping your exposed cartridges into an envelope. (And, of course, paying the tab. That's about $10 per roll of film.) After a trip to the post office, you can sit back and wait for the film to come back.

If you've shot your movie on video or DV, you can skip the processing step—your tape is ready to roll. Watch it on a TV by hooking up your camcorder to the VCR (see instructions in your camcorder manual). You can even watch it directly on your camcorder with the *Playback* function, or on a computer.

Edit Away!

The most common misconception about moviemaking is that a director shoots only the footage she needs. No way. Ordinarily, a director shoots a lot more footage than is necessary for the finished movie. Only a small part of this footage will actually be seen by an audience. And that's basically what editing is all about—selecting and shaping the footage.

The cool thing about making a movie is that it allows you to rearrange a story—you can cut the bad stuff out, or make the good stuff even better. Wouldn't it be great if we could edit our lives that way? Just think: you could get rid of the time you got car sick in the front seat of your friend's car. (You *knew* not to have that double bacon burger.) And then you could replay the time you caught that excellent air on your skateboard. (Nobody believed it later.)

You *can* do that kind of editing when you're making a movie. And if you're really creative, you can doctor your footage to make scenes even more incredible. Like the one in which a crowd of thousands is worshipping you. (Cut Ricky Martin out of the frame, and those people are screaming for *you*.)

And if you use a computer editing system, well, the world is virtually at your fingertips. There are almost no limits to how you can alter your digital footage—change backgrounds, add illustrations, or create new images right on your desktop.

But before we tackle the more complex stuff, let's get the basics down. Essentially, you'll have two ongoing decisions while you're editing:

1. *How long* each scene should be, and
2. *In what order* they should fall.

You do this by cutting and placing your shots together in a sequence of events that makes sense. A lot of editing is about personal taste, so let your artistic vision shine. Learning to edit is like eating chocolate for the first time—once you get a taste for it, it's hard to stop.

Lizzie Borden

"Work on your film until it's finished. It's the greatest thing and nobody ever gets that. I taught myself how to edit and I've never been one of those 'neat' editors. But I love the process—it's about control."

Director **LIZZIE BORDEN** *had the guts to "jump into the void" when she edited her first film,* Born in Flames. *This radical sci-fi drama took her four years to make.*

And when Lizzie finished, she'd created an unflinchingly original movie that critics and audiences widely praise today!

"I used any camera I could get my hands on. I shot once a month over years, working fly-by-night. I couldn't afford to pay an editor, so I did it myself. It was a great way to know my own footage and discover what my film was about."

Rita Gonzalez

"Start really small. Think microcosmic in terms of production so you can get a grip on the process. Editing even a five-minute piece can take months of time. Especially if you work like me—in the head and à la brava."

RITA GONZALEZ

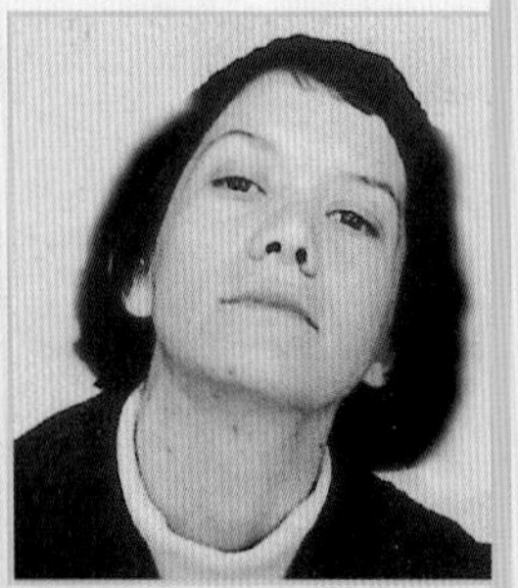

Rita is a videomaker, writer, and curator. Her video movies have screened at various art museums and international festivals. She also curated a survey of media arts from Mexico called Mexperimental Cinema *and the* Joanie4Jackie *compilation,* I Saw Bones.

(see p. 95 for more on Joanie4Jackie)

Here Are a Few Great Things that Editing Allows You to Do:

Choose your take.

If you made a few versions of each shot, now you can choose which one to use in the final version of the movie. Even further, if you like only *part* of a single take, you can isolate it and use it with parts of other takes. For instance, suppose one of your actors messed up her final line at the end of a shot, but everything *before* that was perfect. Rather than redo the entire shot, you can re-record just that line. Then you can edit the second take into the first one during post-production.

Shoot your movie out of sequence.

The editing process allows you to shoot your story out of order—that way you can plan your shots according to other criteria. The biggest one: *location*. If several different scenes use one location, it's probably a good idea to get all the shots you need there, all at once. That's especially true for something like a restaurant, which you can probably use only once. As long as you know how to edit, it doesn't matter that one shot takes place halfway through the script and another at the end. You can rearrange your footage later.

And now that you're not a slave to sequence, you're free to arrange your shots around another important element: *lighting*. So you can shoot all of your daytime scenes on one beautiful sunny day, even if those scenes are years apart in your script.

Tell separate stories in one movie.

You've seen this story device a thousand times in Hollywood flicks. The movie starts with one character (say, *Sal*) and begins to tell her story. Then it cuts to another character, (say, *Herbie*), and begins to tell his story. The two stories parallel one another, until eventually Sal and Herbie meet and the movie is about *their* story. (Think *You've Got Mail* or *Slacker*.)

Another version of this technique is called *intercutting*. It works like this:

- Open on a shot of one character (*Herbie*) drinking a coffee alone.
- Cut to an unrelated shot of a different person (*Sal*) leaving work after a long day.
- Go back to Herbie who's now scrounging through his pockets for cash to pay for his cappuccino.
- Go back to Sal, who's in her fancy convertible, driving through the gates of her estate.

The two characters haven't been on screen together, but by using this intercutting technique, you've created an implied relationship between them. You've given the viewer a sense of anticipation about their eventual meeting, or at least about the connection between them.

Take events out of real time by slowing them down or speeding them up.

Say you want to show Emily walking from school to the local mall. In real life the mall is a thirty-minute walk away from the high school—do you really want to bore your audience with thirty minutes of *real time* walking? (Here's a hint: NO.) Instead, you can simply show Emily beginning her walk (shot 1); and then perhaps the mall sign (shot 2); and, finally, Emily's arrival at the entrance (shot 3).

Here's another example: Suppose there's an important party sequence in your script. You recorded a real party because you didn't have the resources to stage a fake one. (Plus your mom practically had a seizure when you asked to invite 200 people over. Gee whiz.) While you were shooting the shindig, you were cornered by Mr. Chatty from gym class and couldn't reach the camera to shut it off. But all you need for your movie is a few shots of the party. By editing the extra stuff *out* and using short takes of the actions you want, you can accelerate that two-hour party to just a few minutes of valuable footage. That's just enough for your audience to get the experience of the party, without having to sit though the entire thing (not to mention Mr. Chatty).

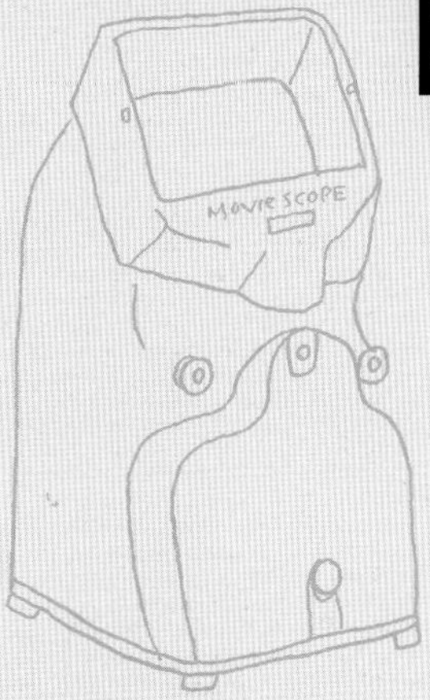

A Moviola, used for old-time editing.

An Editrix's Guide to Easy Editing

I hope I've convinced you that editing is SUPER cool, and you're now wondering how to start cutting your flick. Before you start chopping, take a few minutes to review these four easy steps.

STEP 1

Get to know your raw footage.

Before you start editing, you've got to know your *raw* footage like the back of your hand, so watch it. Don't rely on your memory bank alone! Keep a written log of all the shots, including how long they are, the composition of the frame, and the actions they include. Note cards, post-it notes, or even just a pad of paper will do.

STEP 2

Get choosy.

After you've logged all of your shots, refer back to your storyboard: Do you have all the shots you need? If not, you've got two options—scheduling a reshoot or making do with what you've got through creative editing.

Next, begin choosing which shots you like best by considering lighting, composition, and the quality of your actors' performances. Separate the shots you like from those that you can do without.

STEP 3

Cut your movie on paper first!

Now you want to arrange the shots you like on paper, *before* you start cutting your footage. If you've used a separate note card for each shot, this part will be easy—simply arrange the cards in a sequence that fits your story. If you didn't use note cards, take your shot log and a pair of scissors and cut out the good shots. Spend some time rearranging your shots on paper to get an idea of the different ways you can tell the same story.

STEP 4

Start cutting.

Once you better understand the structure and sequence of your movie, you can begin editing the actual footage. There are SO many different ways to edit your film or video. They range from the really simple (which requires little more than a camera and a VCR) to the super complex (which usually involves some sort of computer-based editing program). On the next few pages are a few different ways to cut and mix your flick. →

"When you are editing you can't fall in love with your work. When a scene or a shot doesn't work, you've got to throw it out."

LESLIE HARRIS *(see p. 31 for more on Leslie)*

This is important, so pay attention.
You've got to know how you'll be editing your movie before you shoot even one frame of your flick. Why? Because how you record or film your footage affects what you can do later during the editing process.

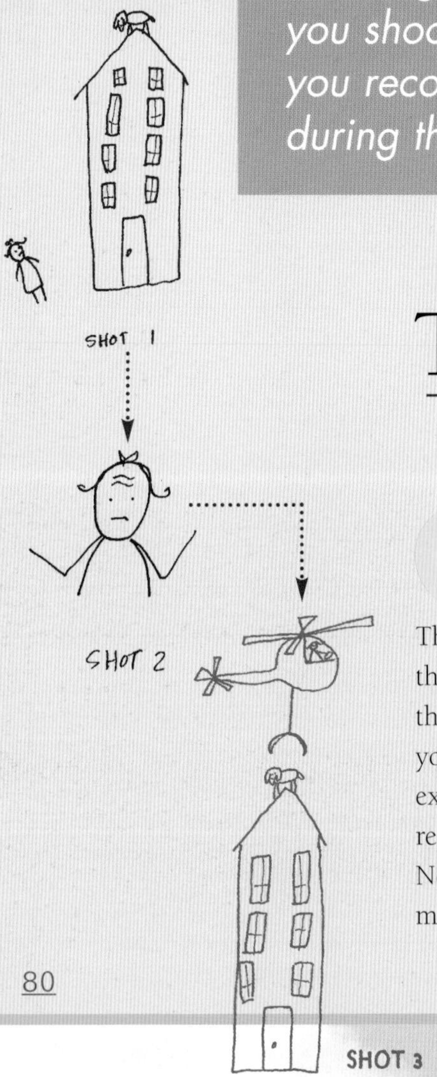

In-Camera Editing

This method of editing works for any format you shoot—film, video, or digital video—and, essentially, it's the *non-editing* way of editing your movie.

Umm, excuse me?
What's that supposed to mean?

Okay, I'll lose the riddles. If you use in-camera editing, you'll actually edit your movie WHILE YOU SHOOT IT. The entire editing process takes place within the camcorder or film camera. That means there's basically no post-production process—you simply film or record your entire movie in exactly the right sequence. Whatever you record on camera is what the audience sees. No cut and mix, no rearranging shots, and no multiple takes allowed.

The major advantage of in-camera editing is that it only takes a camera—no other equipment needed. It is the simplest and cheapest way to edit a movie. The disadvantage, of course, is that you've got to get everything right (and in the right order) the first time. There's no time to add effects and switch around shot takes. Also, you have to shoot your entire movie based on the sequence of the script, or storyline. It's a tough order, but a great option if want to finish your movie quickly.

"Making your first film is difficult. The 2nd film is even more difficult. But the 25th is very difficult. To be a director takes long, patient, and passionate love."

LINA WERTMÜLLER

Not only is she one of the premiere directors of European cinema, Lina has inspired generations of other women directors who love her outrageously funny, astutely political movies. She is the first woman ever to be nominated for an Academy Award as Best Director. Don't miss her films—especially Swept Away, Seven Beauties, Love and Anarchy, Sotto, Sotto, *and* Ciao, Professore! *(All titles are English translations of the Italian originals—so if you can't find them in your video store, get an Italian dictionary and ask again.)*

Lina stays busy behind the camera. Of course, to make over 25 movies in one lifetime, you've got to be working on movies most of the time. As Lina wrote in her interview for this book, "I have endless stories to tell you, but I have to rush off to work!"

Lina Wertmüller

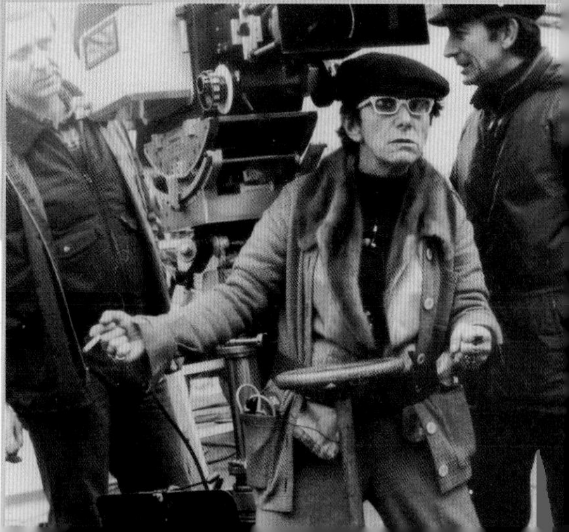

Tape-to-Tape Editing

If you've shot your movie on video, you can edit it with a VCR and television. And girl, this is *easy*. Simply connect your camcorder or DV camera to a VCR. (Your camcorder should have come with the cords for this hook-up.) Use the TV as a monitor so you can see what your transfers look like. By using the *Pause* and *Record* buttons on the VCR you can transfer particular shots from your camcorder's tape to the blank tape. Here's how:

1 Stick a blank VHS tape into the VCR and record 10 seconds of black. Press *Pause*. This will ensure a clean start for your movie.

2 Run the raw footage of your movie on your camcorder by pressing *Play*. When you come to a piece of footage you want to transfer to the blank tape, press *Pause* on the camcorder. This is your "edit-in" point.

3 At this point you have the camcorder's and VCR's *Pause* buttons ON. Now—release both at the same time. The VCR will record the selected footage you've picked.

4 When you reach the end of the shot you want recorded, press *Pause* again on the VCR and stop the camcorder. This is called the "edit-out" point.

A cinch, right? Now, you'll repeat this process for every piece of footage that you want to be in the final, edited version of your movie. After you transfer a shot or scene from one tape to the other, you can check to see how well it transferred by rewinding the VCR tape and watching it on the TV.

Even for a five-minute movie, editing tape-to-tape will take some time—hours, probably. But those hours will fly by as you see your masterpiece taking shape!

Transferring Super 8 Film to Videotape for Tape-to-Tape Editing

Using Super 8? No problem! You can still use tape-to-tape editing by transferring your Super 8 film footage to a videocassette. All you need is a camcorder and Super 8 projector. Once you have your processed film back from the lab, thread it into the projector and play your film onto a white wall. While the filmed images appear on the wall, record them with a video camcorder. Be sure that your camcorder is steady. (A tripod or a tabletop are absolute *must haves*.) You'll also want to frame just the filmed images—you don't want any excess wall to appear in your final footage.

Note: You may notice a *scrolling* effect when you play back the video transfer. *Scrolling* is due to the different speeds at which the film is moving—i.e., the difference between the Super 8 and the videotape speed. (Since video records at 30 frames per second and your Super 8 film is running through the projector at either 18 or 24 frames per second, the images you're recording from film to video will be out of sync.) If this happens to you, refer to your camcorder's manual to change its shutter speed.

If this do-it-yourself method is not for you, any lab can transfer a film to a videocassette. If you pay them, of course!

"Be fearless in your editing. There's a place for everything. Outtakes make for great packing material."

Martha Colburn
(see p. 107 for more on Martha)

Some methods of editing take longer than others. For instance, actually cutting film is a slow and deliberate process, whereas computer editing allows you to edit quickly. In any case, take the time you need to get it right. Your audience will thank you for it later.

Cutting Film

If you shoot your movie on Super 8 film you can edit the old fashioned way—by actually cutting the film by hand.

If you decide to edit on film, you'll need to scrounge around for some gear:

- **a Super 8 editing machine** (called a viewer), and
- **a film splicer.** Your best bet is to check with whomever you bought (or borrowed) your Super 8 camera—they may have the editing equipment too.

A Super 8 viewer allows you to move frame by frame through your film. It's a bit like a primitive, hand-cranked projector, but rather than projecting the image across the room, you see it on the small viewer. Here's how it works:

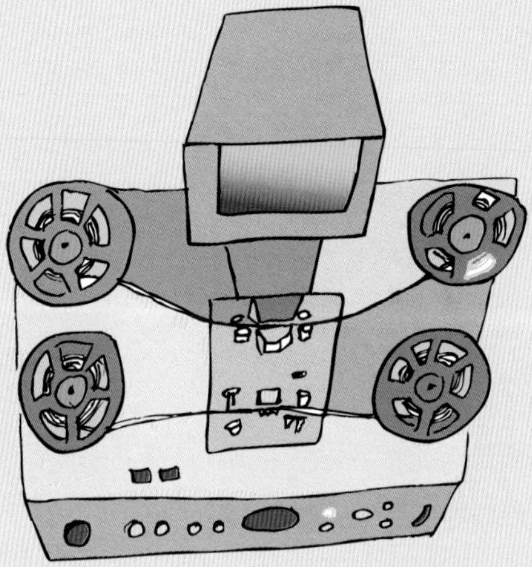

Flatbed Editor
(used for editing large format film)

1 Position your unedited film on the *take-in reel* (on the left-hand side), thread the film leader through the viewer (there are arrows on the machine showing you how), and into the *take-up reel* (on the right-hand side of the monitor).

2 Turn the machine on (plugs right into the wall) and look through your film footage, frame by frame. Once you've decided where you want to edit, you'll actually cut the filmstrip with your handy *splicer*:

3 With your splicer placed in front of the viewer, grab hold of the film, pull it out of the viewer and place it on the splicer. The splicer is outfitted with little spikes that fit the film's perforations, so you can make a clean cut. (Your splicer should also have a razor-sharp blade.)

4 Cut your film into sections by repeating this cutting technique. Then you can label your cut filmstrips with a post-it note and hang them on a wall.

When you have weeded through your entire film and cut out all the mistakes, you can begin splicing scenes together.

5 Again, fit the two strips you want to connect into the splicer by securing the film's perforations to the spikes.

6 Then tape the two pieces together using the special tape that comes with any splicer (or is available in most camera shops). If you mess up on your splice, simply peel off the tape and try again. By repeating this process, you've reconstructed an edited version of your entire film—by hand!

Super 8 editing machine (or viewer)

*For more information on editing Super 8 film by hand see "The Art of Splicing" article on the *Small Movies* Web site, *www.city-net.com/~fodder*, or check out the Super 8 resources listed on page 33 and in the Resource Guide on page 120.

Computer Editing

Whoa, there's been a digital revolution in the editing room—and the revolution is NOT over. From the big studios to no-budget small fries (that's us and we're proud of it!), it seems as if everyone is editing on a computer these days. New software programs can modify the home PC or Mac and turn your bedroom into a full-service editing suite. But until now, you had to have major bucks to buy the stuff.

But don't get me wrong—nobody's giving these computer programs away for free. So how will you get your hot little hands on it? Well, computer editing might be as close as your computer lab at school; or (if you can get the software) your own PC or Mac. Many new computers even have video editing software preinstalled, like the iMovie program on some Apple computers.

The absolute coolest part of editing on a computer is that you can add all sorts of nifty visual effects to your footage. Need to get rid of a misplaced prop? Not a problem! How about adding sound effects? Coming right up! Or is a certain shot too dark? Hey, lighten up! Check your software program for the effects that it includes. Just be careful not to get carried away with the bells and whistles at the expense of your story.

And remember! **Anything on digital video (whether you shot on DV, or transferred film to video) can be edited on a computer, provided you have the right video-editing software.**

Walk away for a while.

If you begin to feel unsure of yourself during the editing process *(Will that shot really work? Should I make the cut here? Which sequence works best?)*, stop editing for a bit and come back to it later. You'll have a fresh eye and new ideas. And it never hurts to ask a friend for her opinion.

Bronwen Hughes *Walked Away Big-time*

"I did my first film, 'Harriet the Spy,' and Steven Spielberg saw it. It was one of those things that only happens once in your life—if you're lucky. He called me to the set of 'Jurassic Park 2' and drove me around in his golf cart. He told me how much he liked the film and that he would love it if I came to make a film at his studio.

"Of course, I was flabbergasted after that meeting. To this day, I've still never formed an entirely intelligible sentence in his presence. But I didn't want to do another family film. It was a painful time because he was sending me scripts and I was passing on them. I was passing on Steven Spielberg and I was unemployed! I would have these moments when I would picture myself waking up in a cold sweat as a poverty-stricken 75-year-old saying, 'And I could have worked for Steven Spielberg.' "

Waiting for the right script worked for Bronwen. Steven finally sent her a script she loved and she directed Forces of Nature *for his studio, DreamWorks.*

COOL CUTTERS

Since the early days of moviemaking, editing has been overlooked as a creative art. And so have the fantastic female editors who've practiced it. Working outside of the spotlight, often alone in dark cutting rooms, these women have been ignored for too long. Get to know a few of them now:

Dede Allen

Simply put, Dede Allen reigns supreme as one of America's most distinguished editors. She has cut countless movies for the most celebrated directors, been nominated for two Academy Awards and developed signature editing techniques. And like all visionary film pioneers, she did it her way—with hard work, tenacity, and a healthy refusal to follow the rules.

A teenager in the early 1940s, Dede was dying to direct movies, so she got a job as a messenger girl at Columbia Studios. There she learned everything she could about moviemaking and earned her way into the cutting room by "carrying more film and swearing more than anyone else, until the men accepted me for the job."

After she made her way into the editing room at Columbia, Dede decided to break more rules, and quit the studio to work as a freelance editor. It was during these freelance gigs for directors like Robert Wise (*Odds Against Tomorrow*), Arthur Penn (*Bonnie and Clyde*), and Warren Beatty (*Reds*), that Dede began experimenting with technique. She created shock cutting (quick cuts with wild contrasts) and audio shifts (overlapping audio from one shot to the next). Her work on these movies set a new standard for rapid and nontraditional editing which continues to influence movies (especially music videos) today. The best news about Dede Allen? She's still at work—and who knows what she'll come up with next.

A few of her more recent movies include: *The Breakfast Club, The Addams Family,* and *Wonder Boys.*

Women assemble film prints scene by scene at Biograph Studios in the early days of moviemaking.

Margaret Booth

Margaret Booth's film career spanned 62 years and her innovative editing techniques have left their mark forever. In the early 1930s she was one of the top editors at MGM Studios and developed new editing styles using sound, color, and wide-screen technologies. Just a few of the classic films she cut: *Mutiny on the Bounty, Romeo and Juliet,* and *Camille.*

Margaret began her career as a secretary, but advanced in the ranks to become the studio's supervising film editor from 1939 to 1968. (Not bad for a dame from the typing pool, huh?) Her creative style as an editor influenced every flick MGM made during those years. In 1977 she was awarded an honorary Oscar for her "exceptionally distinguished service to the motion picture industry."

Verna Fields

Verna was another talented editor who worked her way up the hard way. She began her career cutting low-budget movies and TV shows like *The Lone Ranger*. She was eventually the Vice President of Feature Films at Universal Pictures. Wow!

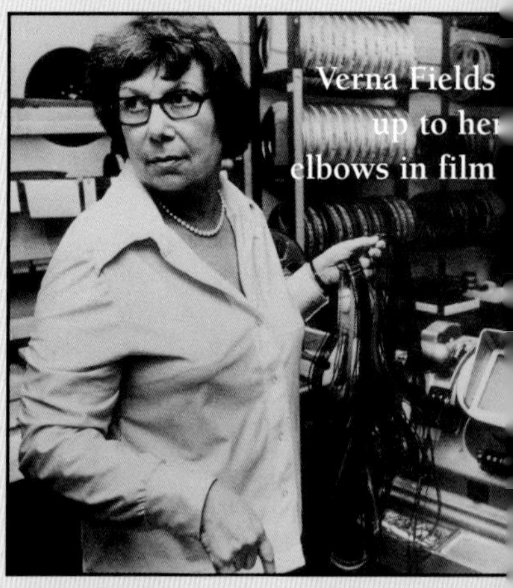

Verna Fields up to he elbows in film

After teaching editing to a few young, aspiring

Sound Off, Rock Out, or Get Funky

Add Music to Your Movie

Try to imagine movies without music—no ba . . . bababa, baba *BAAA BAAA BAAA* in *Star Wars*, no **DU-DUT** bass as the great white shark closes in on some poor surfer in *Jaws*. No soundtracks, period. Celine Dion's career would be *over*.

Music is an essential element of any movie—and not just the ones with a theme song sung by Celine. Music intensifies the viewer's connection to the story and provokes an emotional response. Think, for instance, about the creepy sort of music that foreshadows an on-screen murder. Or the rockin' sounds of an intense car chase, or the sad, lonely tunes that go with a funeral march. Music sets the mood of a film, from the beginning of the movie until the credits roll.

Deciding what sort of music you want in your movie is an important part of the post-production process. After all, even the silent films had music!

On that topic—if you've shot your flick on silent Super 8 film (or on video without sound), you can add music at the screening. It's easy—simply play a CD on the stereo (or cassette or vinyl record, if you're the Old School type) along with your film as you project it. Another option is to have live music accompany your movie, like your friend who plays the cello, or a local band. In that case, be sure the live performers rehearse with the movie running before the screening—that way they'll get the dramatic timing right.

Remember that your sound doesn't have to be limited to music. You can always record a voice-over narrative or dialogue to go with your images. Just use a plain old cassette tape and play it along with your movie.

"I love music. For me, music ties things together and allows an audience to connect with each other."

Barbara Kopple

(see p. 26 for more on Barbara)

directors, Verna helped one of her former students, some kid named George Lucas, by editing his film, *American Graffiti*. Then she persuaded Universal to distribute it. You might also remember a certain great white shark that she had something to do with—she edited the movie that's kept thousands of scared swimmers out of the ocean for years, *Jaws*.

Thelma Schoonmaker

Perhaps the most renowned collaboration between an editor and a director is that of Thelma Schoonmaker and director Martin Scorsese. Their creative partnership, which has lasted more than 30 years, has produced groundbreaking movies like *Raging Bull*, *The King of Comedy*, and *Kundun*. The two met while studying film at New York University and have been working together and inspiring one another ever since.

Although she is most acclaimed for her work on Scorsese's films, Thelma has also worked with other top-notch moviemakers, like Allison Anders (*Grace of My Heart*) and Mary Ellen Bute (see page 106).

Like Dede Allen, Thelma is hard at work on her next movie, so be on the lookout for her next masterpiece. You'll see what good cutting is all about.

"Never underestimate the importance of a good sound recordist."
STACY COCHRAN
(see p. 53 for more on Stacy)

HERE'S A TIP: If the sound on your movie ends up being lousy, turn it WAY DOWN and pretend you always meant to make a silent movie.

© Copyright Blues

You'll find one gigantic obstacle to your super-cool soundtrack: copyrights. All of the songs on the radio, or by your favorite artist are most certainly copyrighted. Don't monkey around with copyrights. Your movie can be barred from screenings if you don't have the legal permission to use a particular song. Getting clearance to a popular song usually takes lots of time and cash. Instead, you be the DJ and create your own original tunes, or collaborate with someone more musically inclined.

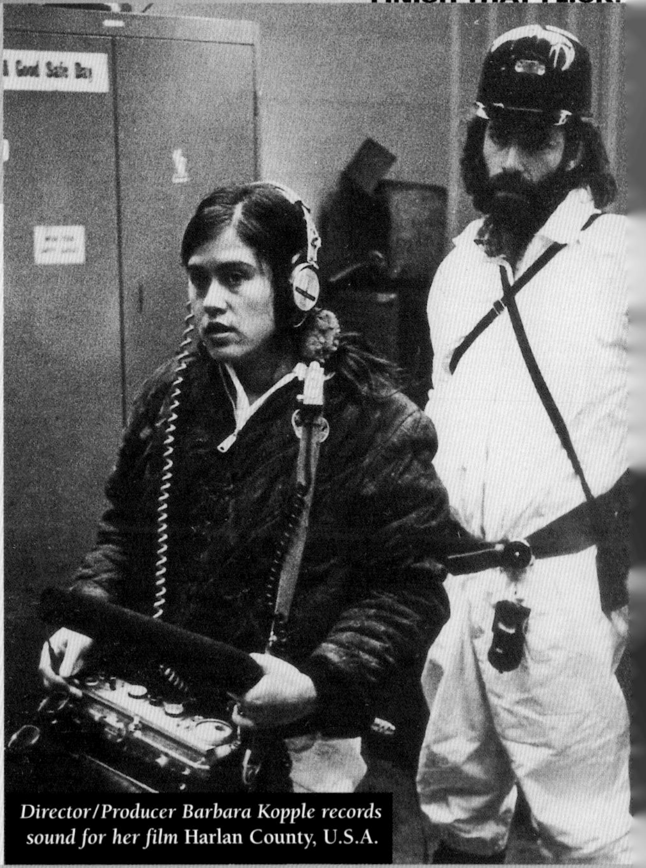

Director/Producer Barbara Kopple records sound for her film Harlan County, U.S.A.

When you're craving a little inspiration, look no further than the nearest video store!

Picks of the Pros

French director Agnès Varda—her movies are must-sees!

"*Vagabond* by Agnès Varda is a film that really stuck with me. Amy Heckerling's film *Fast Times at Ridgemont High* and Martha Coolidge's *Valley Girl*. I saw those movies as a teenager and thought, hey this is the way to go. I also like early Kathryn Bigelow movies. But there are so many amazing women filmmakers out there making interesting movies—Claire Denis and Sofia Coppola, just to name a few." **KARYN KUSAMA**

"*Lady of the Jewel Box* directed by Michelle Parkerson. And Maya Deren, she made wonderful films." **CHERYL DUNYE**

"I remember being really affected by Susan Seidelman's *Desperately Seeking Susan*. Seeing that movie was the first time I walked out of a shopping mall theater and actually felt I'd just seen a movie from and about a woman's point of view. It was the first mainstream movie that really inspired and energized me that way. I love Penelope Spheeris's *Decline of Western Civilization* documentaries for their entertaining perspective on the subcultures of punk and metal. Amy Heckerling creates girl characters with mainstream appeal in films like *Fast Times at Ridgemont High* and *Clueless*. I admire Leni Riefenstahl for the formal brilliance of her propaganda documentaries, which she directed, wrote, produced, and edited. Allison Anders's *Gas Food Lodging* was another film where I walked out of the theater feeling totally validated. I also admire Martha Coolidge, Tamra Davis, and Gillian Armstrong." **HELEN STICKLER**

"Chantal Akerman—I love all her films. I admire *Jeanne Dielman* the most, but was most moved by *Meetings with Anna*—it's a very vulnerable, honest view of a filmmaker's life." **Britta Sjogren**

"Some of my favorite films by women include: *Clueless*, directed by Amy Heckerling; *Big*, directed by Penny Marshall; *The Piano* directed by Jane Campion; and *A New Leaf* directed by Elaine May." **Nora Ephron**

"*Desert Hearts*, that was a great film directed by Donna Deitch. Mira Nair's film *Salaam Bombay!* because it's so moving. And Susan Seidelman's *Desperately Seeking Susan* is great fun. *Born in Flames* directed by Lizzie Borden was the first feminist film I ever saw. Marleen Gorris's films *A Question of Silence* and *Antonia's Line*. Anything directed by Kathryn Bigelow, the royal-action babe, because she's so individual in her choices." **Gurinder Chadha**

"*Watermelon Woman* directed by Cheryl Dunye, *Drylongso* directed by Cauleen Smith, *I Like It Like That* directed by Darnell Martin, and *Boys Don't Cry* directed by Kimberly Peirce." **Lizzie Borden**

"I love Lina Wertmüller's movie *Seven Beauties*—it's shocking, political, angry, and very powerful." **Jocelyn Moorhouse**

"*Boys Don't Cry* renewed my love of cinema. Considering this was a true story and a horrifying one, I felt the director Kimberly Peirce showed the highest respect for Teena Brandon's memory." **Esther Bell**

"I think Lina Wertmüller is an amazing director. Her movies are funny, passionate, smart, cynical, and sexy." **Amy Heckerling**

"My first powerful influence was Lina Wertmüller—her film *Swept Away* is incredible. When it came out it blew everyone's mind. Her work was so fresh, bold, and exciting. At the time it defied what anyone expected a woman director to do." **Maggie Greenwald**

Lina Wertmüller

"There are so many films by women directors that I admire especially movies by Clarie Denis, Chantal Akerman, and Jane Campion. See anything you can by these women and also seek out more experimental directors like Peggy Ahwash, Leslie Thorton, and Abigail Childs." **Catherine Hollander**

Crazy for Jane Campion!

"*The Piano* by Jane Campion and *Swept Away* by Lina Wertmüller. Because I love them." **Stacy Cochran**

"All of Jane Campion's work, but especially *The Piano*. Every image burned itself into my brain. I also love *An Angel at My Table*." **Lizzie Borden**

"*Angel at My Table*, Damn, I thought that was a great film! I watch it over and over again. I watched it before I made *Private Parts*, basically before I make every movie, I try to watch it again. Jane Campion's a great director—the acting is impeccable. I love that movie." **Betty Thomas**

"I have a huge affinity for *Angel at My Table*. Jane Campion has stubbornly made her way and never once been boring. I remember seeing that film at the New York Film Festival with a close female friend of mine and during the scene where the sisters dance in princess hats in the blue-lit forest, we both started to cry. There was something about witnessing the power of a girl's imagination, its validity as subject matter that was completely beautiful. It was a short scene, almost a fragment, but it remains vivid to me to this day." **Katherine Dieckmann**

"*The Piano*, directed by Jane Campion for her use of sound and image. *Dance Girl Dance*, by Dorothy Arzner is amazing for that incredible monologue Maureen O'Hara delivers to the male audience watching strippers. And *Meshes of the Afternoon* by Maya Deren (a true pioneer in the field) made me understand the importance of the camera as a part of storytelling." **Bette Gordon**

"Jane Campion's film *The Piano* is one of the strongest films ever to be directed by a woman. It is passionate, powerful, magical, profound, and startling." **Gillian Anderson**

"The early short films by Jane Campion—you can rent them on video now. I saw them in high school and they were so incredible, but also made me feel like I could make movies too. And Alison Maclean's *Jesus' Son*—I learn a ton from her." **Miranda July**

Chapter Eight

Dim the lights, pop the corn, and (finally!), SIT YOUR BUTT DOWN:

Girl Director, It's Show Time!

Ah, your first screening. After all the sweat, fake blood, and real tears (from your best friend, who as it turns out really *can* act), that glorious moment is here. Just think: only a few weeks ago it was a rough idea, and now it's a real thing—a videotape or film reel in your hand. At last you can sit back, relax, and enjoy the fruits of your labors. Of course, a bunch of other people will be there too . . . watching. Watching *your* movie. Will they like it? Will they laugh at the funny parts? What if they don't? (Or worse—maybe they'll laugh at the *sad* parts.)

Wait a minute. This isn't relaxing at all! Just when you thought the panic attacks were over, you've run into a wall of performance anxiety.

Don't worry—this is normal. Even the most experienced directors have these pre-screening jitters. So prepare yourself for some fingernail-biting, wobbly-kneed anxiety. Because if you've made a movie you care about, you'll naturally be a little nervous before its first screening. Keep your cool by remembering that, even now, you are still in control. While you can't predict the audience's reaction you can remind yourself that, to a certain extent, you don't care. You made this movie from a place inside you, and it's a story only you can tell. And that, my friend, is definitely its own reward.

See, it *is* fun to screen your flick. You'll get to watch people laugh, cry, and get mad or scared enough to talk to the screen. When the credits roll, you'll realize you've done something that your audience was moved by. Yep, your movie can truly affect people—from the girl in the back row who told you that something like that happened to her once, to the guy who said your movie changed his life. That feels pretty good, doesn't it? Makes you want to show it some more, eh, Girl Director? And you will.

Here's how—

Irene Turner

"The ultimate goal is not getting your film made—the ultimate goal is getting people to see it."

IRENE TURNER

Irene's directed many short films and recently made her first feature, The Girls' Room. *She also co-produced* Billy's Hollywood Screen Kiss. *Check out her Web site at www.girlsroom.net.*

Show It Off, Girl

SCREENING!
OF MY MOVIE
THE RISE OF PRINCESS CHARLOTTE
MONDAY 7PM!

It goes without saying that you should throw some sort of party after your flick is finished—and what better way to celebrate than by screening your movie for your friends, family, cast, and crew? Hello premiere party! Everyone will be thrilled to see their efforts up on screen, in fully-polished form.

All you need for your movie's premiere is a place to watch it, something to watch it with, and an audience. It's that easy.

STEP 1
Make your own movie theater.

Whether it's your backyard on a warm summer's night, the living room, or your high school auditorium, find a venue that can seat the size of your expected audience comfortably. It should be a place that's easy to get to and *free*. If that last part is a problem, consider charging admission at the door—maybe you can work out a split with the owners.

Some possible venues for your screening include:

A garage or basement. *(Yours or a friend's)* Dark, a little damp, but totally free! Also ideal for access to electricity and the kitchen. (What would a screening be without snacks?) Just make sure your hosts don't mind 20 kids traipsing through the house in search of the bathroom. (Hint: Make signs that clearly mark the quickest path.)

The great outdoors.
Show your movie under the stars and let Mother Nature host your event. A warm night in a backyard or park provides a perfect setting for your screening. Your only challenge will be finding a source of electric power nearby. Tell people that if they bring blankets to sit on and picnic baskets to snack from, you'll provide the entertainment. Project your movie onto the blank wall of a building or house (don't forget to tell the people inside what's going on), and you're ready to roll.

Cafés or coffee shops.
Many coffee shops or small cafes are willing to turn over their space for a movie screening provided you ask many weeks in advance. They will appreciate the upswing in business if your audience likes to stay caffeinated. (Hey, it's also a good way to keep your crowd awake.) Plus, cafés and coffee shops usually stay open late, so their staff won't be working overtime. Another bonus—plenty of chairs and comfy couches for your audience.

Community centers.
From the YMCA to nonprofit art centers, leave no stone unturned in the search for a screening venue. Church basements, Masonic lodges, abandoned barns—anything you can get permission to use (and that has electricity) works just fine. Forget fancy, this is about having fun and seeing your flick.

Art galleries.
Hey, they're always looking for artists, right? That's *you*. Talk with the owner or head curator about donating an evening or afternoon for a video/film screening.

Clubs.
As long as it's approved for the "under-21" crowd, a club is a great place for a screening since there's lots of room. This choice could have drawbacks, though. One is a lack of chairs (try borrowing folding chairs from school). Another is cash—owners will want you to pay

"Pick up a camera and make stuff—that's the easiest advice. And after you make it, you've got to show it to people. That's kinda the hard part—show it to people and don't worry about pleasing everyone in the room. You don't want to. Listen only to what the audience you've made the movie for has to say. If you made the movie for 14-year-old girls and they love it, but some 40-year-old man doesn't, who cares what he thinks!"

Tamra Davis
(see p. 49 for more on Tamra)

Tamra on the set of her film Skipped Parts *with actor Jennifer Jason Leigh.*

Karyn Kusama

"Get in touch with that part of yourself that says your voice is important. Because I don't think the public reaches the filmmaker. I think the filmmaker has to reach the public with her specific, singular vision of the world. I hope that is true, otherwise I'm in trouble."

KARYN KUSAMA

Karyn's writing/directing debut film, Girlfight is a fierce story of a quick-tempered girl who finds self-respect and love in a boxing ring. A boxer herself, Karyn's personal experiences inspired her to explore the nature of fighting and adolescence in this movie.

to use the venue. Try to make a deal with them—maybe plan a Saturday afternoon event (when the club's usually closed). Or be more creative—team up with a local band for a mixed-media extravaganza and split the costs.

And, oh yeah, real MOVIE THEATERS.
Maybe one of the movie palaces in your town will allow you to hold a one-night screening of your flick. Ideal conditions, yes, but it's usually hard to find a theater willing to show "unknown" work. (*Yeah—just you wait.*) It's a long shot, but it never hurts to ask.

STEP 2
Get the gear you'll need.

A Projector System:

For VIDEO: A television set (with as big a screen as possible) and a VCR. For larger venues, you might be able to snag a video projector.

For FILM: A Super 8 projector. If you can't find one to borrow, check out the thrift stores again, as well as the local classified ads and camera shops. Maybe they'll let you rent one just for the night of your premiere party. Although it's best to find a more permanent set-up, since you'll probably want to watch it more than once, right?

A Screen:
If you're using a TV, you've already got the screen. If not, try to find a freestanding screen—sometimes you can even check one out from the library. Or use an old white sheet or a clean white wall. Or get creative like filmmaker Melinda Stone (see page 94 for more on Melinda) and project your flick onto a bed of white flowers at night!

A Stereo or Portable Boom Box:
You'll want this equipment if you've got a silent movie with a musical soundtrack or voice-over. It's also festive to have some music playing in the background of your event before and after the movie. This *is* a party after all.

Extension Cords:
Keep a few of these handy fellows around because the cords on your equipment are never, ever long enough to stretch to the nearest outlet.

Transportation:
You'll need someone with a car to give you a lift to and from your screening location. Even if you can drive, you won't want to haul all that stuff by yourself.

A couple of good friends:
(Preferably one with the car, right?) Depending on how big you make your screening, it'll be good to have a few friends around for moral support, and to make sure everything flows smoothly.

STEP 3
Invent your audience.

Decide who your first audience should be—do you want a closed event, with just friends, family, the cast, and crew in attendance? Or do you want to open your premiere to the public (provided you've got the space)? For a smaller, private premiere, make sure you've invited everyone who's helped from the *best girl* to the nice clerk at the camera store who sold you two videotapes for the price of one. A personal invite to see your film will mean a lot to the folks who helped you out. It's a good way to say *Thanks*.

Work That Projector

Of course, if you're screening your video for 20 pals in your basement, a TV/VCR set-up will do the job perfectly. A larger venue and bigger crowd might require you to find a video projector and movie screen so that everyone can see and hear the flick. (50 people look silly crowded around a tiny TV set.) And it's just as easy to operate —you simply plug it into the VCR and project away!

If you're screening a Super 8 movie (that hasn't been transferred to video), you'll need a Super 8 projector. All Super 8 projectors have automatic threading, so loading your film into the projector should be a breeze.

Here's how:

STEP 1.
Place the film on the *take-out* reel and turn the motor ON. (But keep the lamp off.)

STEP 2.
Feed the film leader into the projector. The film will pop out the other end of the projector—where the *take-up* spool is turning around.

STEP 3.
Position the film around the take-up spool and turn on the projector's lamp. A bright beam will come on, and your images should appear on screen.

Super 8 projectors are more fussy than video projectors—but honestly, it's not their fault. Since Super 8 films, unlike videos, are actually cut and spliced together in the editing process, there is always the possibility that a sloppy splice or torn sprocket hole will jam the film. Here's the worst-case scenario: the image on screen suddenly freezes and begins to burn. (For those of you lucky enough NOT to know what this looks like—it's when your carefully composed, beautiful image suddenly becomes a brown melting circle.) TURN OFF THE PROJECTOR IMMEDIATELY. But don't panic, your entire film has not been ruined—usually only a frame or two has been burnt—cut them out, and you can splice the film back together later.

One more note: If you're not too overwhelmed on the big night, run the projector yourself. It's a good feeling to see the movie completely through, start to finish.

Helen Stickler

"Carry a lot of confidence, you need it."
HELEN STICKLER

As a filmmaker, Helen has written, directed, and produced two award winning short films, **Queen Mercy** *and* **Andre the Giant Has a Posse.** *She's hard at work on more movies.*

If you want *more* people to come, send out invites, including mass e-mail. And advertise your show by placing flyers in local hang-outs—your school cafeteria, video stores, music clubs, book stores, and restaurants. If you're planning a HUGE event, consider charging admission. It may be a set ticket price or a donation jar at the door to cover your costs. (*Note*: Admission doesn't always mean cash. You could, for example, ask people to bring canned goods to donate to a charity.)

In fact, your screening can be an entire business venture if you plan carefully. If you don't charge admission, maybe you can run a snack bar and cover expenses by selling Junior Mints and popcorn (all the necessities!). If you *do* charge admission, make sure you have more on the program than a 3-minute movie. Go as far as you want to with the business angle of your premiere, but don't get sidetracked from the main point—*to get your movie seen.*

If you do decide to go all out, *alert the*

media! Send local newspapers, television, and radio stations an announcement of your movie event. Who knows—they might show up, or at least give you some free press. Keep any clippings that make the news for your files. They'll come in handy when you're raising cash for your next movie.

STEP 4
Have fun and thank the people who come.

No matter how stressed you're feeling at your screening, take a minute to look around the room at everyone who showed up. Out of all the things these folks could be doing tonight, they're here to support you and your movie. Why? Because they believe in you and what you do. That, Girl Director, is better than any amount of money you can make.

At some point during the event, pass around a notebook for names and e-mail addresses—that way you can keep in touch and invite them to more screenings, let them know about your next flick, or just send them a personal *thank you* for showing up.

Besides turning the VCR or projector on and finally sitting your weary behind down in your chair, that's all you need to do for a great screening. Repeat the process as soon as you make your next flick. That audience will be ready for more.

"You're not a filmmaker until people see the movie. Distribution is important to me because I'm not going to let history pass me by—I want to change things and get my thoughts out there—you can't do that unless you get your movie seen!"

SARAH JACOBSON *(see p. 49 for more on Sarah)*

"Write thank you notes." **STACY COCHRAN** *(see p. 53 for more on Stacy)*

film festivals

Another way to get your movie seen is to send it off to various film festivals. Most major cities have some sort of short film and video festival—some cities have *many* festivals, all with different themes or interests. Start by researching festivals, focusing on those that seem appropriate for your movie. The Web is a great resource, as is talking with other moviemakers.

Submitting your movie to a festival requires familiarizing yourself with the entry requirements, and sometimes paying an entry fee. Entry requirements usually cover the format, length, or theme of your movie. As for that entry fee—well, you've already spent cash *making* your flick—don't break the bank sending your movie to a bunch of festivals. Select only a few that seem right for your movie. That cash is better spent investing in your next movie anyhow.

Film and video festivals are a great way to find a larger audience, and your movie can travel to all sorts of places you've never been. People all across the world can see your movie, without it costing you anything but postage. And if you *are* lucky enough to attend the festival screening you can meet lots of people in the moviemaking biz (Schmoozing 101!). You'll also get to see amazing movies that you won't see anywhere else. And as for awards, it's an honor just to be selected, so anything else your movie wins along the way is bonus. It's fun just being there—everything else is icing on the cake.

FIND A FESTIVAL FOR YOUR FLICK

Check out page 120 for a short list of some super cool film/video festivals. But don't just stop with my favorite picks—there are thousands of festivals out there (and more every year!)

D.I.Y. Be a Festival Founder

But wait a second—why wait for someone else to screen your work when you've already figured out that you can do it yourself? Girl Director, nothing gets by you. I like where you're going with this . . . *why not start your own film festival?*

Holding your own film or video festival isn't any more complicated than holding your premiere screening—except that you gather together other D.I.Y. moviemakers to show their work too. Circulate the word that you are looking for films or videos to screen by posting flyers around town, and by handing them out at other film screenings. (You could even start a Web site.) Recruit people for your festival committee and hold a meeting to discuss your various goals. Decide when and where it will happen, and get to work securing the things you'll need—a large venue, equipment, and publicity.

Since most of the submissions to your festival will likely be from no-budget moviemakers just like you, expect the movies to be short (under 15 or 20 minutes). That means that you'll need about eight to 10 films for a two- to three- hour show. Make the festival interesting by mixing it up a bit—screen animated movies, documentaries, music videos, dramas, even home movies. Ask all of the directors to introduce their shorts, with you as the "emcee."

As with your screening, try to drum up some free publicity for your festival. A few months before the scheduled event contact the local media—radio, TV, magazines, and news-papers—and tell them about the festival. (You'll want to write a simple press release. Include information about the movies that will be shown and the directors who've made them.) Offer interviews and contact numbers to press people who want to talk with you or other members of your committee.

If your festival is a success, why not make it an annual event? (Or if you're *really* ambitious, a monthly one.) Soon you'll be at the center of an entire moviemaking community.

Making VHS copies of your movie is also a good way to fund your next production. Sell copies of your movie and use the profit for your next movie. It's like a bake sale, right? Only you're selling something that's *really* good for people.

Distribution: Have Mailbox (or Inbox), will travel.

If you can't take to the road yourself, you can always send your movie out on its own. If you have access to a computer, you can post it online or send it out via e-mail. Or you can always go the snail mail route, and distribute your movie through your local post office. That means you can send your movie just about anywhere. Here's how:

1. Using a VCR, copy (dub) your movie from the original tape to a pile of blank videotapes. (Or you may be dubbing a compilation of short movies from a group you've formed.) Label the contents and set the tapes aside until you decide who the lucky recipients will be.

2. Research film/video groups and festivals in the U.S. to find that fortunate recipient. (Postage adds up so be choosy!) Write or e-mail them first, to find out if they're interested in screening your flick. If you've started your own festival screenings, ask them about trading programs. (For example, you could sponsor a screening of movies from Chapel Hill, North Carolina; and a group in Chapel Hill could return the favor by screening your movies.)

3. Continue to search for people, places and groups you'd like to send your extra dubs to and ask them to send you theirs. That way you'll spread the wealth of girl-made movies around the globe (or at least around your state).

The SUPER Super 8 Show

Rogue road advice from Melinda's movie, "Visionary Environments and Amateur Adventures":

- Check oil, tires, and brakes
- Talk to local folks
- Attend regional pie tastings
- Take the back-roads over the interstate
- Stop when you feel the urge, you might never be here again

Imagine a perfect night of movie watching—great films, interesting moviemakers, good conversation, a breezy night, an occasional sing-along, and live music. Now you've got an idea of what it's like at the *Super Super 8 Festival,* and chances are it's coming somewhere near you soon. And if you're *really* lucky you'll meet founder **Melinda Stone**, a moviemaker and Super 8 aficionado. A true take-charge gal, Melinda decided to create her own film festival as a way to get her films shown and to promote the work of others. Hence, the *Super Super 8 Film Festival,* an annual festival on wheels that screens small-gauge short films (Super 8 and 16mm).

And just how far does this party travel? Around the world. Yep, I'm serious. And so is Melinda. In fact, she and the band of traveling filmmakers who take the *Super Super 8* across the globe each year are so serious about getting folks out to see (and make) Super 8 films that they'll do anything to attract an audience—bingo games, dancing, performances—heck, even giving away Super 8 cameras and film as door prizes. The *Super Super 8 Festival* beautifully captures the can-do spirit of D.I.Y. movie production by promoting audience participation and screening experimental, highly inspirational short flicks submitted by filmmakers around the world (and selected by an eclectic jury that sometimes includes Melinda's mom).

So be on the lookout for a faded blue van (which is outfitted to sleep three bleary-eyed festival makers) coming through your town soon. Or take your cue from Melinda, and start your own traveling show.

Melinda Stone

Melinda on the road with filmmaker friends and festival helpers Kate Haug (see p. 72 for more on Kate) and Vera Edelson. Melinda is a professor of media studies at the University of San Francisco, an outdoor cinema impresario, and an occasional documentary filmmaker. You can see her movies on www.insound.com

"I love presenting my work and the film work of others in outdoor settings with live music—and lots of activities like bingo and sing-alongs. I love creating events for films."

MELINDA STONE

OR Go On-line!

Make a Web site for your movie. Many sites offer free space for Web pages, so find a server that's right for you. Then build your site, including a brief synopsis of your movie, still photos from the shoot, and descriptions of your cast and crew. I love sites where the director includes storyboards and even journal entries from her production journal—it really puts the audience behind the scenes. If you want to get fancy, add a clip from your movie using a software video player (like QuickTime or Real Player)—or post the whole flick. That way folks can see your movie online. Instant access = instant audience. Make sure your audience can e-mail you, or add their address to a log, so you can e-mail them.

Joanie4Jackie

Girl Director, check out the coolest thing around in movie distribution. She offers "medicinema for what hurts." Her prescription? Watch more movies made by girls. Girls just like you, who have a one-of-a-kind story to tell. And Joanie4Jackie makes sure WE get to see them.

Miranda July, performance artist, avid moviemaker, and the legend behind Joanie4Jackie has been distributing lady-made movies since 1995.

Joanie4Jackie is a hit—12 video compilations of lady-made movies are already available, and Miranda says there's no sign of slowing. She takes to the road regularly with her tapes, screening them at all sorts of venues and carving out a space for more renegade women-made movies. (Oh—and somehow she manages to find the time to make great movies *herself*.)

Because, as Miranda says, *The bottom line is that no one is going to make your movie but you.*

Check it out: *www.joanie4jackie.com*

The first Costar tape.

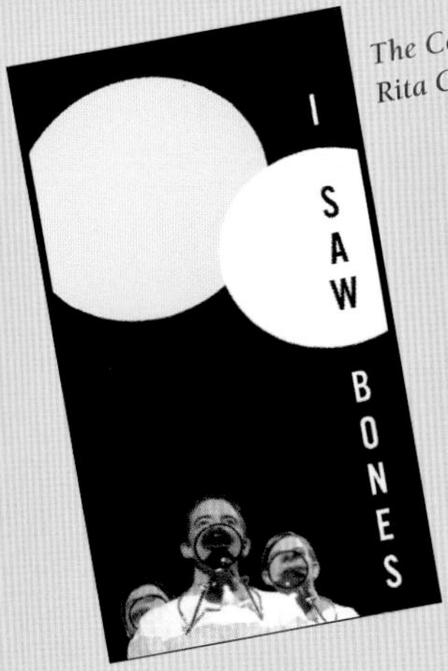

The Costar tape curated by Rita Gonzalez (see p. 78).

Your heart is on a videocassette—now what do you do? Send it to Joanie4Jackie and Miranda will put it on a chain letter tape.

Miranda July

From Miranda:

"My fantasy was to have a correspondence course for girls who wanted to make movies, where it wouldn't matter where you lived or how old you were. So I made this pamphlet up saying that it's a challenge and a promise—you make the movie, I'll distribute it. So when a band was playing or something was going on in my town, I'd pass these pamphlets out. Very slowly, months and months later, the first 10 movies came in. Every time I got one in the mail, I'd get really excited. And when I had 10, I made the first tape."

Heather Rose Dominic

"There is such a luxury in committing a story you've created to film and seeing it actualized. I can't imagine being in any other business!"

HEATHER ROSE DOMINIC

Heather directed and produced The Shield Around the K*— a documentary about K Records. Her next film is a punk rock Western.*

Chapter Nine

Animate This!

What do Bart Simpson, the Powerpuff Girls, and Scooby-Doo have in common? They are all brought to life through *animation*. And cartoons are only the beginning: By experimenting with different techniques you can give life to just about anything. Drawings, clay sculptures, magazine cut-outs—any object you've got lying around can move! (And let's face it: sometimes inanimate objects can be easier to work with than actors.)

That's because rather than just *record* motion, an animatrix (that's a grrl animator) actually *creates* it. That's the main difference between *live action* (the type with human actors) and *animation*. In a live-action movie, every movement you see onscreen, from Brad Pitt's poster-boy smile to the swing of Xena's battle-axe, was made by an actor and then captured by the camera. The movements in an animated movie, on the other hand, don't really exist—they're an illusion created on screen through the recording of pictures in rapid succession. The "movement" is created by slightly changing each drawing.

Animators may also use still *objects*, like clay figures—slightly changing the position of the figure for each frame (à la *Wallace and Gromit*).

Too many people think animation = Disney flicks—where teams of animators work together for years to create the thousands of drawings necessary for a feature film. But animation comes in hundreds of different forms: cartoons on TV, commercials (Hello, *Tony the Tiger*), the Internet, and hand-painted films. And it definitely doesn't have to be a big production: animation can be made anywhere (provided there's a flat surface) and with a *very* small team of, well, one. (*That's you!*)

In the early days of movies, short animated films were called "curtain raisers" and were shown before the featured film. Now you can find short animated movies almost everywhere *but* big movie theaters. (Sadly, they've gone the way of real buttered popcorn.)

But guess what—you can make your own curtain raisers! So go ahead and make two spoons do the jitterbug, use your old toy soldiers for a soap opera, or crash land that UFO using paper plates and string. Girl, if it's around, you can make it *move*.

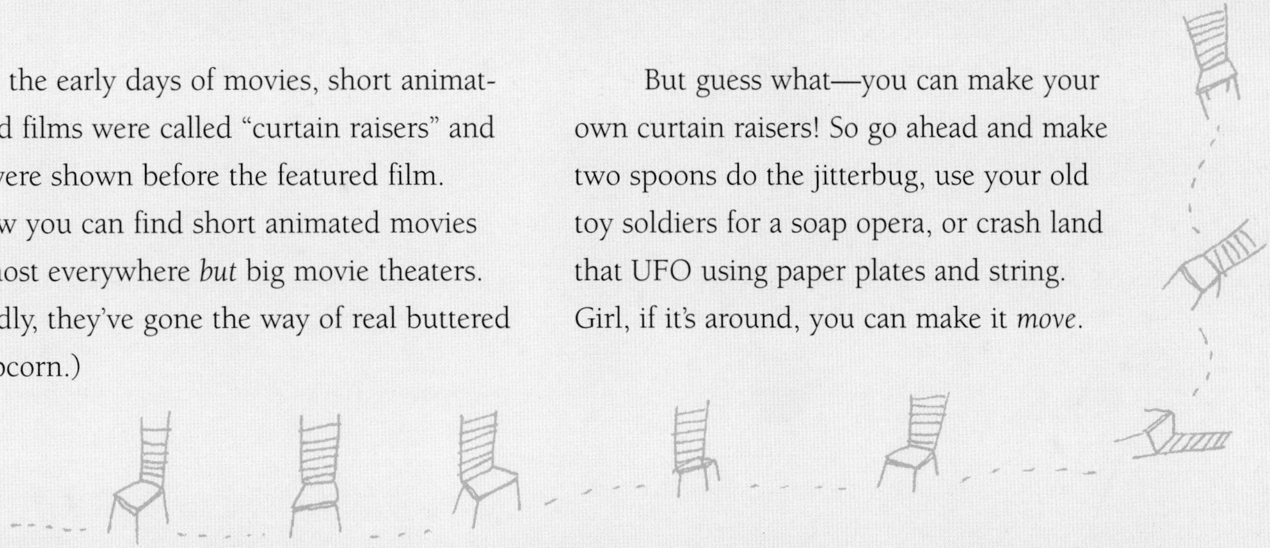

Animate This! Exercise: Flipout Over a Flipbook

The quickest way to understand animation is to make a *flipbook*. See the image in the corners of this book? That's a flipbook. It's a collection of small drawings or pictures bound together in book form. Each drawing is slightly different from the one before it. When you flip through the pages quickly the drawings appear to move.

(Of course, maybe you've already done this in the corner of your school notebook. Yeah, you sure *looked* like you were taking notes in Biology.)

What you need:

- A pencil or pen
- A stack of large note cards or blank paper
- A big rubber band

Any movement can be the subject of your flipbook—a shape, a stick person, or a cartoon character. Start drawing a figure on a single note card or slip of paper.

Say, for instance, you want to animate a girl doing a cartwheel. Start by drawing her standing up. Then, on the next piece of paper, draw the same figure in the same part of the page but with a slight difference. Maybe she's stuck her foot forward in the next picture. And in the next drawing, she's got her arms extended. Next draw her halfway to the ground, and so on.

You get the idea, right? (Draw on the lower half of the note card or piece of paper so there's enough room to bind all your drawings together later.) Each successive picture should be more advanced in the movement than the drawing before it.

When you've finished all your drawings (it takes a bunch—about 50 or so drawings will make a two-second flipbook), stack them together in sequence. Then bind them together with a rubber band. Now's the really snazzy part: flip through the book quickly. The single drawings now look like a continuous movement.

What you've just done with your flipbook is moviemaking in its most basic form. You've successfully made a blank page come to life—with nothing but a pen and paper!

What It Takes to Be an Animatrix

To make an animated movie, you'll need the same basic equipment as for other types of movies:

- A camcorder, DV camera, or Super 8 camera
- Videotape or film
- A couple of desk lamps
- A tripod (essential for animation!)

And then there's some additional gear to find:

An animation board

An animation board, or stand, is any flat, steady surface where you can place the artwork or objects you want to animate. A tabletop works just fine, so try the kitchen table or your desk. Usually, I use the floor and a piece of black cardboard. *Tip: Make sure you can sit down. Trust me, it takes some time to make an animated movie and you don't want spend it on your feet.*

FYI: The Techie Stuff You Need to Know

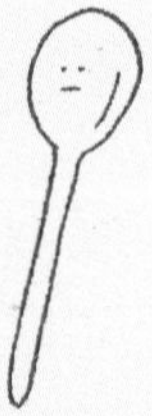

If you're using a video camcorder . . .

Some camcorders have fancy gizmos designed especially for animation. Check to see if yours has an *interval timer* (sometimes called an *intervalometer*) or an *animation facility.* Both of these cool extras enable you to record very short takes. The interval timer allows you to get a "mini-shot" (record for just a second or two when you press the *Record* button. If your camcorder has this feature, set it to record only a few frames at a time (4–8 depending on your camcorder).

If your camcorder *doesn't* have any of these animation features, don't sweat it—you can still make an animated movie. You'll simply get your "mini-shots" by pressing *Record*, and then *Stop* (or *Pause*) as quickly as possible. It's not perfect, but it still makes cool animated flicks. If your camcorder has a remote control, that's a major bonus since it means you don't have to touch (and inadvertently move) the camera. So if you've got a remote, use it.

If you're using a DV . . .

DV cameras usually have a "still photo" feature that records a short shot automatically. If your camera's got one, use it to make animated movies. Then edit the stills together later, and *Presto,* you've got a movie. Or you can use the same start-and-stop technique mentioned above.

If you're using a Super 8 . . .

Super 8 cameras are perhaps the best equipped for animated movies because most can film a single frame at a time. (Just look for the switch—it's usually on the side of the camera and can be set to film 1, 18, 24, or 36 frames a second.) If you can't find the switch, look for a socket to attach *a cable release.* This cord controls a button that fits in your hand, and when pressed, advances your camera a single frame at a time. Cable releases are great because they eliminate camera jitters—once you've got your camera in position on the tripod, you never have to touch it again as you film.

(Note: If you decide to buy a cable release, be sure to take your camera to the camera store to find one that fits properly.)

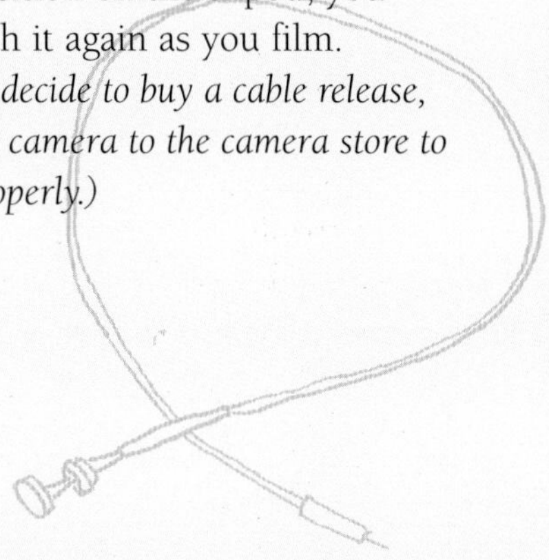

Stop-Motion Techniques

The process of animation is basically the same no matter which camera or format you use. You're recording (or filming) a few frames at a time, using a technique called *stop motion*. After you record a few frames, you'll stop the camera and move the object you're recording slightly. In this manner, frame by frame, you'll create the "action" of the object.

Quick Stop-Motion Tips:

1. ***It's all about the motion.*** The story is important in animation, but remember to stay focused on the movement of your subjects. So before you begin, pay attention to the movements in the world around you. Observe how people walk and talk. Note how facial expressions and body language reveal emotion. You can base the movement of your objects on human motion, and within a couple of frames, your audience will feel empathy for a pea or a tin can.

2. ***Keep the actions broad.*** That way they will register well on camera. Too much detail on your drawings (or the choice of an elaborate object) can confuse your audience and detract from the overall effect of your movie. Try to capture the *essence* of the movement, rather than showing every tiny detail.

3. ***Use simple backgrounds.*** You don't want too much going on in the background of your animated flick—it takes away from the main action of the subject's motion.

4. ***Keep that camera still.*** Once again, use that tripod!

5. ***Shoot more than just a single frame at a time.*** With a camcorder, this is a given, since you won't be able to record single frames. But with a DV or Super 8 camera that takes single stills, go ahead and shoot 2–4 frames for each motion. The movement on screen will still be super smooth, and your film will be longer.

Feeling empathy for a tin can

Finally, be creative. Once you get the hang of it, animation allows you a lot of room to play. Make your own rules!

Tina Bastajian

"Break the rules, follow no recipes, and nurture creative accidents."

Tina Bastajian

Tina is an experimental film/video artist whose work has screened in festivals worldwide. Her movies explore memory, language, identity, and the relationship between these themes. Her films and videos are available from www.canyoncinema.com.

Awesome Animation Ideas

As with any movie, the first step is coming up with IDEAS. What do you want to animate? An object? Or a series of drawings? Once you start looking, almost everything around you is a potential subject for your animation.

Artwork

Any series of original drawings, paintings, or doodles can be turned into a movie using *stop motion* animation. Just number the pages, tape them down one by one, and record. One variation on animating original artwork is *cel animation*. That's where an artist draws on clear transparencies so she doesn't have to redraw the background elements for each picture.

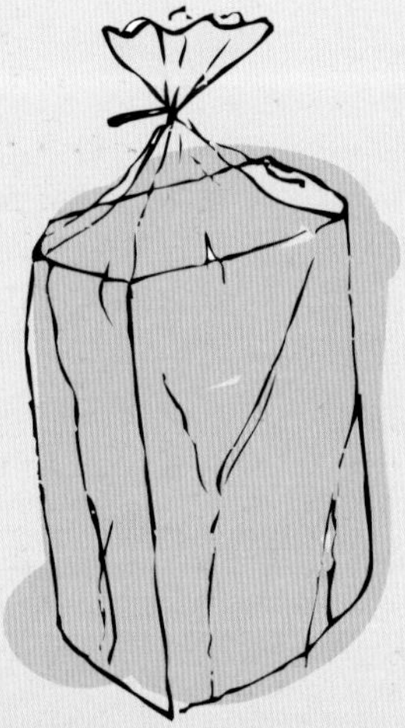

Clay

Claymation uses clay figures as the subject of the movie. (Think *Wallace and Gromit*.) You can create your own characters from clay or Sculpey (available at any art supply or hobby store). If you're new to the world of clay molding, some handy tools you'll want to find are *a roller* (to flatten out the clay so you can work with it), *a knife* (for cutting the clay), and some *toothpicks* (for adding small details like eye sockets).

Cut-outs

Make paper figures, or cut out pictures from magazines, and you've got more great subjects for an animated movie. Cut-out animation is fun for a beginning animator because it's a quick way to get fast results. That's because you're using *found footage*, rather than drawing everything yourself.

First, decide what you want to use as a "character"—maybe some cut-out cars, or animals from a magazine. (You can make your own character by drawing one on a piece of paper, coloring it, and cutting it out. Or cut out a picture of yourself and be your own star!) Then pick out a picture from a book or magazine to be the background scenery. To animate your cut-out, tape down the background picture, then move the cut-outs on top of the scenery.

If you want to get fancy with your character's movement, add hinges to the underside of the figure so you can make its arms, legs, and head move. Use sewing thread and masking tape to attach different body parts to the shoulders and hips. Or to make your cut-out figures *really* expressive, draw eyeballs and different sizes of mouths on a separate sheet of paper and cut those out too. Then you can change your character's facial

If you don't want to buy clay, but want to give clay-mation a try—improvise. My mom offers Girl Directors everywhere her special recipe for homemade "clay":

- **1 cup flour**
- **1 cup water**
- **1 tablespoon vegetable oil**
- **1 teaspoon cream of tartar**
- **1/2 cup salt**
- **food coloring of your choice (4–6 drops)**

Mix all ingredients in a large pan. Cook and stir over medium heat until dough pulls away from the sides of the pan. Remove from heat and let cool. Knead 5 minutes. Store in an airtight container. When you're ready, animate your baked goods!

expressions as she moves.

Food

Animation is a great excuse to play with your food. Expose the undiscovered athleticism of a carrot, or if you want an ensemble cast, tell the story of an entire salad's marathon race. Don't forget to include the dinnerware as well. Remember that dancing spoon I mentioned earlier? It's a sure winner for the 40-yard dash. *Warning: Choose a subject that doesn't rot or turn brown too quickly! (Unless you want your movie to be about mold growth.)*

Photos

Use still photographs for backgrounds, or cut them up (just as you would magazine pages) to create new subjects to animate. Or here's another option: gather snapshots from your most recent vacation (whether it was to the Bahamas or your friend's house) and record them one at a time—for just a few seconds each. You've got a short movie version of your trip—cool!

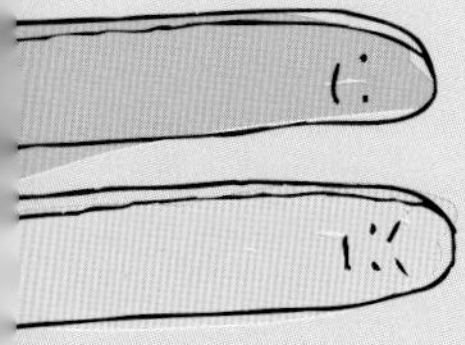

Puppets

Puppets can be made out of anything—wood, wire, cloth, or felt. Heck, even Popsicle sticks and old socks can make plucky puppets for you to bring to life.

Toys

In your movie, that old rag doll could teach GI Joe a thing or two about throwing a punch. Or those little metal racing cars could make a great high speed chase (à la *Thelma & Louise*). In fact, any old toys from your closet could make great animation subjects. Especially since many toys contain moveable parts—stuffed animals, action figures, or even the cheap toys from a Cracker Jacks box—the possibilities are limitless. Think

2D vs. 3D

The set-up for animating a 2D object (like drawings or photos) differs from that for 3D objects (like puppets or clay figures). Instead of pointing your camera down at the drawings (or other 2D objects), you'll film 3D objects just like you would people—straight on horizontally. That means instead of having a background beneath the subject, it will be behind it. Say, for instance, you want to make an animated movie of the TV remote control crawling across the living room and wiggling in between the cushions of the couch—you won't need an animation board. You'll aim the camera straight on, just as you would film a "live action" subject.

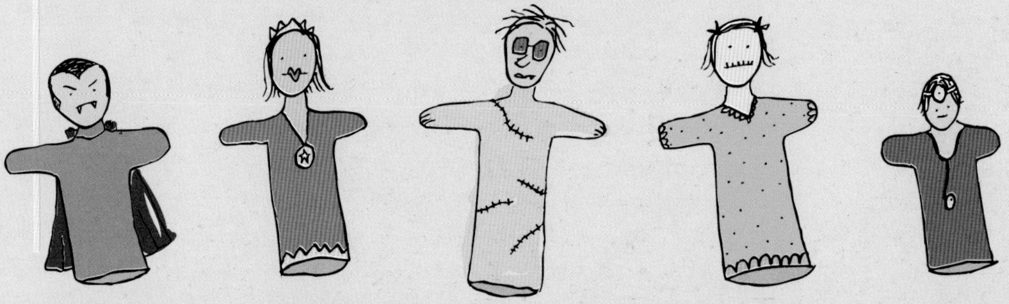

Action,

Maggie Greenwald

"The most essential quality to do anything—especially filmmaking—is the desire to do it, the joy in doing it, and the tenacity to keep doing it no matter what."

MAGGIE GREENWALD

Maggie writes and directs all her films, including her first feature, Home Remedy, *a film noir* The Kill-Off, *and a radical Western,* The Ballad of Little Jo.

Maggie on the set of Songcatcher, *which received a standing ovation at the Sundance Film Festival and won the Outstanding Ensemble Performance award.*

Step 1:

Prepare your camera.

Load the videotape or film into the camera. If you're using a Super 8 camera, attach your cable release onto the camera.

Step 2:

Adjust your animation board and background.

In order to keep your drawings or objects steady as you record them, attach a piece of cardboard to the top of the table. (You can do this with clips available at any hardware store.) That way your drawings will stay in place. If you're animating a flat subject, like drawings, you might also want to draw guidelines on the cardboard.

If you want a background, draw it yourself, or use a photo or ripped-out page from a magazine. Or use a sheet of blank paper for an easy, clean background.

Step 3:

Put the camera in place.

Attach your camera to the tripod and point it directly down at the cardboard frame (or toward the object you're animating). Focus the lens manually by zooming in as close as possible to your subject. Then, zoom out and frame your subject the way you want. If it's still out of focus, move the camera higher (or lower) until it is in focus.

Step 4:

Shed a little light on the subject.

Set a tabletop lamp on each side of the animation stand to light your artwork evenly. If the lamps have adjustable heads, set them at a 45-degree angle to your cardboard frame. (If you're using a camcorder, you'll probably have enough natural light.)

Step 5:

Hit that *Record* button (or film trigger).

With your flat drawing or 3D object in focus, carefully (without moving the camera) press the *Record* button. (Ideally you'll have a remote control for this part.) Or, if you're using Super 8, click the *cable release* button. (Go ahead and click it twice, remember?)

Animatrix!

Step 6:

Stop and change the motion.

Hit the *Record* button on your camcorder (or remote control) again as soon as you can. Make your shots as short as possible (under a second is great). When your camcorder is paused and no longer recording, or after you've pressed the cable release button twice, you're safe to move on. (Switch your drawing to the next picture, or move your object into its next position.) Remember to make these adjustments *slight*, so that the movement will flow.

Make sure the object or drawings on your animation board are in the right position. Unless you've moved the camera out of its original position, your focus should still be okay. (If you want to check it, carefully look through the viewfinder without touching the camera. Or if your camcorder has an LCD screen, rotate it so you can watch as you animate). Then get ready to set your timer again to record.

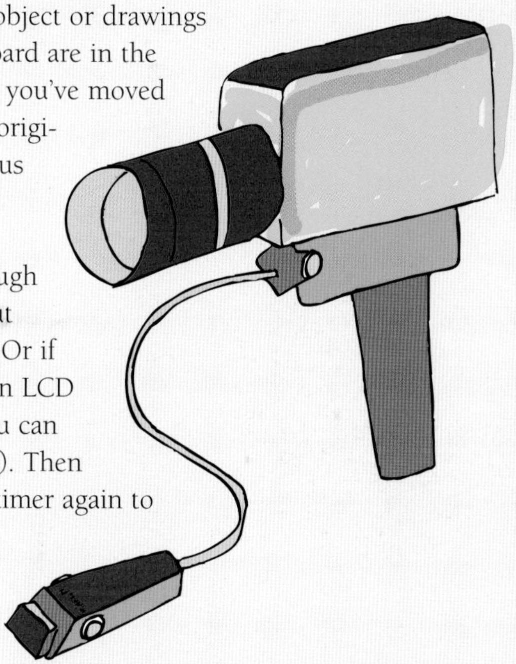

Step 7:

Repeat, repeat, repeat.

Repeat this process until you've recorded every page of your artwork or the entire action sequence of your object—a few frames at a time, of course!

Step 8:

Watch your objects or drawings come alive on screen!

As you know, if you've shot on video, you can pop it in the VCR or play it back on the camera to view your animated movie. If you're not happy with it, re-record. (One drawback of Super 8: you have to wait until after the film has been processed in a lab.)

Animate This! Exercise: TURN YOUR FLIPBOOK INTO A MOVIE

Using the stop-motion technique you've just learned, record or film the drawings from your flipbook. To do this you'll need to remove the rubber band and place the pictures, one by one, on your animation board. Record each drawing for a few frames. When you finish, you've made an animated movie. It's that simple. Wow!

ANIMATION ABOUNDS

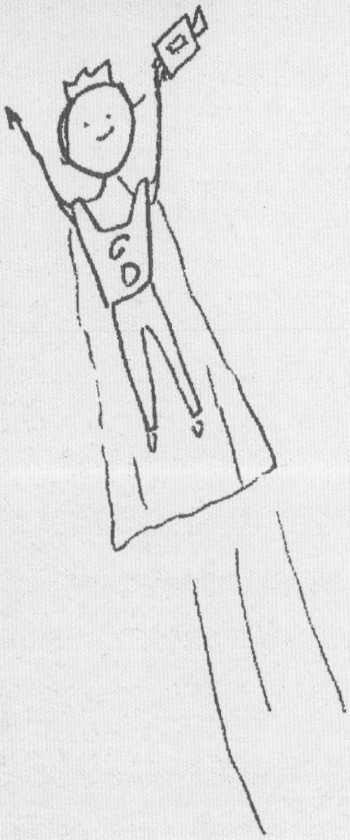

Looking for more groovy ways to use animation? You've perused the recycling bins and cut up every magazine in the house and you're still looking for subjects. Here are more ideas for the animatrix who can't stop:

Pixilate people! Why should a sock puppet or a tin can have all the fun? You can use stop-motion animation on *human* subjects too, by recording them in various fixed poses. The lucky actors will dazzle your audience with some astonishing (seemingly impossible) moves.

The Slinkster Slide

Recruit a pal to stand in front of your camera with her feet together. With your camera steady on a tripod or a tabletop, set up a long shot of her in profile. Record a quick shot. Then, ask her to take a step forward. Record again. After every quick shot, ask her to take another step forward. Repeat until she moves out of frame. Play it back when you're done and, guess what, it looks like your friend effortlessly slides across the ground.

The Invisible Car

This move is similar to the slinkster slide, except that your friend starts by sitting down with her legs stretched out directly in front of her. Record her movement with the stop-motion technique—guess what she does now? She glides across the floor on her butt.

Fly Girl

Even better, make your friend *fly*. Ask her to jump in the air at the same instant that you press the *Record* button on and off. (Or that you click your cable release.) Repeat this over and over, and she'll *whoosh* across the room just like Superwoman.

Pop Goes the Girl

People can "pop" in and out of your movie with this technique. It's easy: record or film a few frames of your subject in front of the camera, stop recording, have them move out of the picture frame, then resume recording. With this effect, you create the illusion that your pal has disappeared.

Magic Box

For this trick, you'll need a few more friends—say Liz, Maria, and Teena. Place a large cardboard box in the center of your camera's frame. Record a few frames of Liz climbing out of the box and walking off screen. Stop the camera and ask Maria to hide in the box. Now record *her* climbing out of the box and walking off screen, just like Liz did. Now do the same thing with Teena. When you play back your movie, it will look like all three girls were in the small box at once.

Tree Transformation

This effect is a variation on the "Magic Box." Record someone walking across the frame of your camera and going behind a tree. When the character is hidden behind the tree, stop recording and have a *different* person hide behind the tree. When you resume rolling, have her come out from behind the tree for a switcheroo. Way funny.

Time-Lapse

Here's another amazing thing animation can do—collapse time. This type of animation is called *time lapse*, and it can change the speed of natural events by slowing them down, or speeding them up. Here are some examples:

Flower Power

This is a familiar example of the time-lapse technique. (Remember Germaine Dulac and her lima bean from Chapter One?) Time-lapse allows you to record a plant shooting out of the earth, sprouting leaves, growing tall, and finally blooming into a beautiful flower—all in just a few seconds.

Cloud Covers

Follow an afternoon's worth of cloud movement by recording a few frames of the sky at one-minute intervals for a few hours. When you play back your experiment, you'll see clouds sweep quickly across the sky to reveal the moving artwork of nature.

Magic Pictures

Place a blank piece of paper on your animation board and record a few quick frames. Then start drawing a picture, stopping to record your work intermittently. The playback will reveal the picture "drawing itself," or magically appearing over time.

Terrific Traffic

By setting up your camera near a city street, then intermittently recording, you can reveal amazing traffic patterns. Show an entire day's activity on a particular highway or street corner in only a few minutes.

The exact amount of time between your exposures or shots depends on the nature of your subject. Recording the growth of a flower, for example, may take a week, whereas documenting the construction of your neighbors' house could take a full year.

Book IT

Want to go learn more about animated movies? Check out these great books:

Make Your Own Animated Movies and Videotapes by Yvonne Anderson

The Animation Book by Kit Laybourne

The key to making a good time-lapse movie?

Figuring out the right interval between shots. Just use some common sense—it takes less time for an ice cream cone to melt than for a flower to grow. So if it takes your flower 14 days to bloom, record a few seconds of tape or film twice a day. If your ice cream cone melts in five minutes on a hot sidewalk, shoot a few frames every 10 seconds or so.

Awe-Inspiring Women Animators

Women have been sketching, cutting, collaging, and moving all sorts of animation objects since—well, since it was invented. We couldn't possibly list them all, but here are just a few.

Mary Ellen Bute

Ping-Pong balls, bracelets, and egg beaters—those were just a few of the objects Mary Ellen Bute used to make her animated short, *Rhythm in Light.* From 1934–1959, her 11 experimental films played in theaters around the country and were seen by millions of theatergoers. Sadly, her movies are little known today because few good prints remain in existence.

Formerly a painter frustrated by the limitations of still images, Mary Ellen began making animated movies in the 1930s. She worked with mirrors and firecrackers to create swirling designs that she would then set to music. These abstract works led her to experiment with the *oscillograph*—something that she called her "pencil of light." With this tool, Mary Ellen could generate moving images electronically without the hands-on work that animation usually requires.

Lotte Reiniger

Lotte's career is among the longest and most prolific of any filmmaker in history. From 1919–1970, she made more than 70 movies, and today is best known for her use of *silhouette animation.* Using elaborate paper cut-outs that she made freehand, Lotte used stop-motion to make her intricate silhouette characters move gracefully across the screen. Many of the films she made for children are based on myths or fairy tales—which she would give her own original twist.

In 1923 Lotte began work on *The Adventures of Prince Achmed.* Though she was only in her mid-20s, the success of her previous short films convinced a banker to finance the three-year long production. With a staff of five, Lotte animated hundreds of detailed silhouettes for her story, based on *The Arabian Nights.* By the time she finished, she'd made the world's first feature-length animation film.

Martha Colburn

Martha is a self-taught/self-sufficient filmmaker who began making movies by cutting up, hand coloring, and splicing old films that she found at the State Surplus store for $10. Since then she's made over 35 short films and still feels like "there's 10,000,000 things I haven't explored—film is limitless." And she does it all herself, in her cozy, unheated studio in Baltimore. Martha often tours the world with her films (and sometimes her band, The Dramatics), so be on the lookout—she may come your way. Because, as Martha says, "It's the process I live for. When I'm done with one film my head's onto the next." If you can't see them in a theater, several of Martha's movies are on the small screen at www.ifilm.com.

"The strange and wild things I did as a teen have found their way into my animated films. Use your life experiences—they are essential." MARTHA COLBURN

A DO-IT-YOURSELF GUIDE by.Collage Maniac MARTHA COLBURN.

COLLAGE ANIMATION

First of all,some reasons why collage animation rules!!!!!

1. The world is overflowing with what we use..MAGAZINES!
2. Our characters require no acting ability.
3. We can have friends and famous people in our movies without having to pay anyone for their time.
4. We can have animal stars that would be too dangerous to film.(paper animals don't need to eat and they can't bite!)
5. You can do it at home.

HOW DO I START?

1. gather lots of magazines,paper,glue,paint, and some string.
2. If you want your friends(or yourself) in the movie then take some photos of their faces and cut them out.
3. Now cut out tons of images,hands,legs,etc...
4. Have fun assembling characters or enviroments from these images.
5. Hunt up some backgrounds or draw them.
6. Get a film or video camera.Animation is simply many still pictures (or Frames) seen rapidly.There are (in film) 24 frames seen in one second of time. If you want to avoid the technical oobly-goobly, start by filming 6 frames,moving your subject/character ¼ of an inch,then film 6 frames,then move character etc... A basic formula is:The smaller the movement of your character and the fewer frames per movement ,the smoother the movement will appear.It will be very spastic on the other hand if you film 10 frames and then move your character two inches. It's quite simple and fun to experiment.
7. Watch what you've done and say "WOW!" and do more!

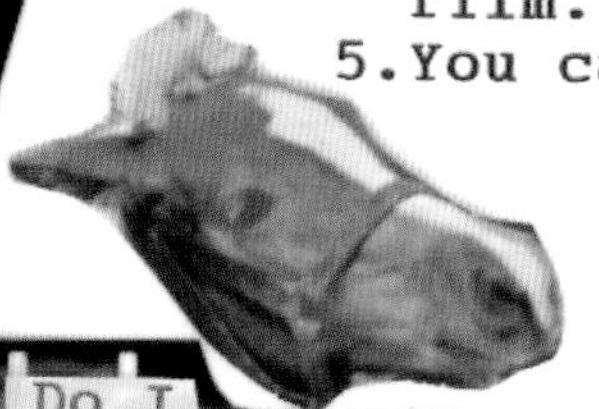

Do I want to be a horse?

A mouth for every mood!

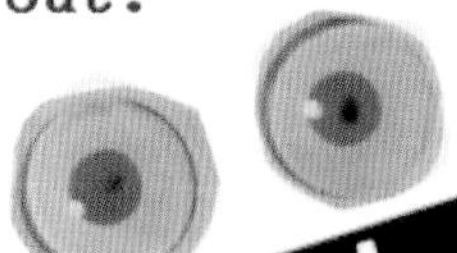

Alien eyes?

optional radio?

The Ghost Feet?

A pet Giant Grasshopper?

Chapter Ten

Mary Pickford with her fans! *(see p. 13 for more on Mary)*

Be a Fan: Start Your Own Girl-Made Movie Community

1. **Pay for a ticket to a gal-made movie (box office receipts talk!).**
2. **If a movie-maker comes to your town for a special film event—GO!**
3. **Start a cineclub. Grab your pals to make and show your own lady-made flick.**

Tricks of the Trade

By now you've got tons of moviemaking know-how under your belt. But how can you give your movie that final finish, or kick it up a notch with a little *panache*? Special effects, make-up tricks, and a few dazzling dupes can *supe up* your picture—all it takes is some creativity, maybe even some trickery. So here are some nifty ideas to add to your bag of tricks.

Tell It with Titles

Titles give a lot of information to your audience quickly. And while titling doesn't really qualify as a *trick*—it's a great way to cheat by getting information on screen without images. You can establish the subject, mood, or location with only a couple of words. Adding titles to the beginning and end of your movie helps to shape the story—think of them as your bookends. Remember, title sequences might be the first and last thing your audience sees, so make sure they are memorable *and* readable.

Many camcorders and DV cameras come with *caption generators* (CG's for short) that allow you to type in text right over a recorded image. Using a CG is fine for simple titles and final credits, but sometimes you'll want to create your own homemade titles.

If you are making your movie through in-camera editing, record the title of your movie as your first shot. But if you're editing the flick together later, you can record titles whenever you want. The easiest way to make your own titles is to write, type, or draw the title on a sheet of paper and record it for a few seconds. As a rule of thumb, you should shoot titles for about twice as long as it takes you to read all the words in your text.

There are a thousand different ways to come up with crafty title sequences. You can cut letters out of newspapers or magazines (for that **RaNSoM NoTe** look), place your letters on top of maps, use picture postcards for a backdrop, or arrange fridge magnets to spell out your title.

Or you can simply record a ready-made title. Look around you—you'll find lots of them free for the taking. Say your movie takes place at a Fourth of July parade. Record the first float that has a sign saying, "Pride in the U.S.A."—how's that for a title? You can use road signs, historical markers, shop marquees—even bumper stickers in exactly the same way. Just keep an eye out for signs that suggest the subject of your movie. If your movie takes place at the beach, write the name of your flick in the sand, and hit *Record* as the waves wash it away.

For creating the title or final credits of your movie, try a few of these ideas:

- Animate the words using seashells, beads, string, paper cut-out letters, or letter tiles from a Scrabble game. Make individual letters *move* across the screen using the stop-motion technique you learned in the last chapter (*remember?*) until they spell out the title of your flick, or the names of your cast and crew.
- Write your titles or credits on a clear transparency and overlay it on a picture, or hold it in front of scenery from your set.
- Buy a set of cheap stencils from a hobby shop and arrange the letters as you please. You can also use a rubber stamp set—heck, you can even craft your title into a temporary tattoo. It's all up to you.

Titles aren't just for the beginning and end of your flick—you can use them anywhere within the movie to clarify changes of location, time, or events. It's called *intertitling* and you've probably seen it used in lots of movies. (Like when suddenly "Five years later" appears on screen.)

Important stuff to remember as you make title sequences: they should be legible, not too wordy, and on screen long enough for the audience to read. There's nothing more frustrating than watching a movie and trying to read a paragraph of text in four seconds. (*Is there a speed-reading course available with the popcorn please?*) Also, don't thank everyone you've ever met in the final credits because it takes too long to watch. (And if it's a short, the credits could last longer than the movie.) You'll have plenty of time to give everyone kudos in other flicks. And the screen credits are *not* the place to let your crush know you care (unless they are super cute and have a really short name).

"There's always something to do even when you're not behind the camera. There is always a way to be working on your film. You've just got to figure it out."

CHERYL DUNYE

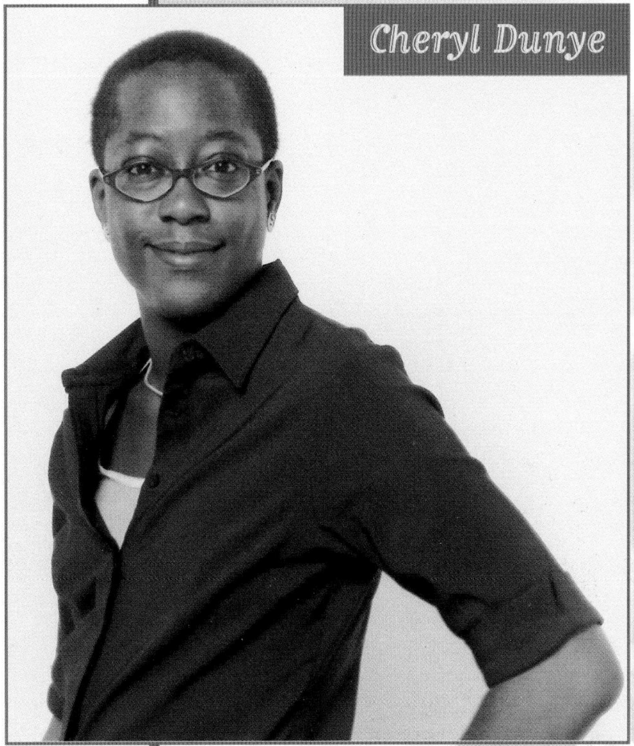

Cheryl Dunye

Cheryl has been making video art for over a decade. Her short pieces include She Don't Fade, The Potluck and the Passion, *and* Greeting from Africa. *Her feature film debut,* The Watermelon Woman *is the first African-American lesbian feature film. She is also a professor of Media Studies at Pitzer College and at work on her next film. Check it out at www.cheryldunye.com.*

Transitions:
Dissolve, Wipe Out, or Just Fade Away?

Allison Anders

"If there's someone whose work you're passionate about, you almost have a responsibility to connect with them. You are never too big or famous to write fan letters!"

Allison Anders
(see p. 1 for more on Allison)

Allison writes fan mail to whoever inspires her. A series of fan letters to German director Wim Wenders encouraged him to see Allison's first movie—a Super 8 flick she made in college. The two are still supporting each others' work—and, 'he STILL has all of my massive volumes of letters that his wife has carefully archived for him!' "

Okay, so transitions aren't really *tricks* either, but they certainly are handy devices to make your movie look more professional. Or to help you get from one shot to the next in a flashier way. These days, transitions are usually added to a movie in the editing phase by computer. You can do that too or create them as you shoot.

Basically, a *transition* is that moment that comes between two separate shots or scenes in a movie. Say, for instance, the movie you're making is a biographical pic about Eartha Kitt*. For the first scene in your movie, you want to show Eartha as a child (let's call that *Scene A*), and then follow that sequence with a few shots of Eartha in concert (*Scene B*). How do you move Eartha smoothly from Scene A to Scene B? Use a *transition* to signal the passage of time.

For instance, you might fade from an image of little Eartha singing as a child to one of grown-up Eartha singing on stage. Transitions are visual clues to your audience that two different scenes are related and that the director is in control of the story's course. And then your audience, like putty in your hands, will sit tight to see where you take them.

There are many types of transitions, and the ability to do most of them is in your camera already. If you're using a camcorder or DV camera, check to see which transition features it has—most camcorders do *fades, wipes,* and *dissolves* with the press of a button. Even with a Super 8 camera, many transitions can be done in-camera while you shoot. (Your job is to figure out where the right button is and when to use it.)

Dissolve

A dissolve is a gradual transition in which one shot fades out as another fades in—for a brief moment you can see both shots on screen simultaneously. Dissolves are used to indicate a location change or the passage of time between scenes.

Fades

Fades are the most familiar transition device—the screen fades to black and the final credits roll. But that's just one way to use a fade—you could also *begin* from black and fade *into* your scene. Or you could fade from your scene into *white*—that's called a *washout transition.* In it, the image simply bleaches out until the screen is totally white. Then a new scene follows.

It all has to do with the amount of light you let pass through your camera's lens—most cameras have a *Fade* function button that will do the work for you.

Jump Cut

Essentially, a jump cut is a "jump" from one scene to the next *without* any other transitional devices. You simply stop the camera after one shot, and then start it again on the next scene. It allows you to group together a bunch of

*If you don't know who she is, you'd better look her up—she's far too cool a cat for you not to know.

quick, disjointed scenes without worrying about how they flow into one another. (Think MTV, and how a video will *jump cut* back and forth between shots of the band performing and a story from the song.)

Wipes

If your camcorder has a wipe feature you can do all sorts of nifty transitions where one shot moves across the screen and appears to "wipe away" the preceding shot. These slick transitions change the scene, but don't slow down the pace of events. Consult your camera's manual for the different ways you can make a wipe move.

NATURAL WIPE—If your camera doesn't have a wipe feature, you can do a natural wipe. Simply use an object to cross in front of the lens (you can also ask a person to walk in front of it), until it's blocked completely. Or cover the lens with your hand (don't touch it though) while you are recording a shot. Then when you are ready for your next shot, start with your hand over the lens, hit *Record* and pull your hand away.

Low-Tech FX

You don't need a million-dollar budget and a super computer to add special effects to your flick. You'll be surprised with what you can do with just the contents of your cupboards. Here are some ideas to start with:

The Weather Report

Need snow for a scene? If you live in Southern California, you have a problem. Well, don't wait around for Mr. Frosty—unless this global warming stuff gets really out of hand, he's not coming in time for your shoot. Take control of the elements and start your own snowstorm. That's right—you can change the weather with the help of a couple of crew members and some goods from the supermarket.

Snow

From painted-white cornflakes (an old episode of *The Brady Bunch* inspired me to try that one—it's great) to styrofoam peanuts, there are endless ways to make fake snow. Or you can buy that stuff in a can that's for Christmas trees, and spray it on your set and actors. Instant blizzard!

Cotton balls, large pieces of confetti made from white paper, feathers from an old pillow—these are just a few of my favorite things. And roll-out cotton sheets (find these in the Christmas aisle) can look just like a fluffy snow-covered lawn.

So once you have your *faux snow* good to go, how do you make it fall realistically? Get a sure-footed friend to stand on a stepladder just above your camera, and let the white stuff fall gradually! Even though your snow is only in the foreground of your shot it will look like it's snowing all over your set.

Rain

Rain works just like snow, only you'll trade in the cornflakes for a garden hose or a bucket of water and a colander. (For those of you who don't know your way around the kitchen, a colander is the thing used to drain pasta—kind of a large bowl filled with holes.)

First, set up your camera on the tripod and spray down your actors with the hose. (*Umm, excuse me, but was this in my contract?*)

At this point you might want to cover your camera or camcorder with a plastic bag so it doesn't get wet. Water will ruin your equipment, so be careful. Position your pal on the stepladder and have her hold the colander out of frame. As you record, have her slowly run water through the colander . . . and *Voilà*—a sudden shower!

Here's a variation on the theme—if you place a piece of glass in front of your camera (and maybe for safety's sake a plastic bag around the camera too), you can shoot a splash of water directly toward the camera.

Wind

An electric fan (and probably an extension cord) are all you need to simulate a windy day. Place the fan just outside of the frame and blow your talent away. Or if you don't have a fan, ask a friend to throw leaves up in the air strategically so they glide past the camera's lens.

Fire

Your entire life you've heard: "Don't play with matches." Well, now is *not* the time to break that rule. So a big warning is in order before you even think about simulating fire. Be careful and smart—fire is dangerous. You are creating an *illusion* of fire—*not* the real thing.

To simulate something burning, place candles or a lighter between your camcorder and the set. Keep the candles or lighter out of the frame so that only the flame appears in the foreground of your shot. Don't let the flame get anywhere near the camera's lens—the heat alone (not to mention the fire) will destroy it. (For safety's sake, if you *do* ever attempt to simulate fire, keep a bucket of water around AND ask an adult to supervise.)

Another safer way of simulating fire is to use orange and red pieces of thin plastic. Cut the plastic into strips and place them below the camera's lens. Then use a fan to blow the plastic strips into flames.

Rachel Talalay

"The great part of working on low-budget films is that you get to do lots of different things."

Rachel got her start in the movie biz as a producer and production accountant for such movies as Hairspray *and* Cry-Baby. *She's gone on to direct* Freddy's Dead: The Final Nightmare, Ghost in the Machine, *and* Tank Girl. *Aside from working on feature films, she's also directed many TV series including* Randall and Hopkins (Deceased), To Have and to Hold, *and* Ally McBeal.

"I worked myself from the ground up in the business. I was working at Johns Hopkins as a computer programmer when I saw this ad that John Waters was making a movie in town. I called up and asked if I could work on it, and they said, 'Do you have a car and will you work for free?' . . . My parents were absolutely beside themselves. I kept saying, 'It's not an X-rated movie, but you know I am working with a female impersonator. A three-hundred pound female impersonator.' "

RACHEL TALALAY

Massive Make-up

Nothing says low-fi FX better than tons of make-up. You can pile it on your actors to create gross looking monsters, aliens, and slasher victims with fake body parts falling off. Bad wigs, fake eyelashes, and temporary tattoos—these too are some of my favorite things. Glitter is great, and so is washout hair dye. Use all of these with abandon and you'll not only have a crazy-looking movie, your cast will be the hit of any costume party. Make-up is great for effects because it's cheap and not a big pain to clean up. (Except for that lead actor who had to cut off her fluorescent green hair. *Whoops . . ..*)

Make-up ideas? How about fake freckles, moles, black eyes, or missing teeth? And let's not forget scars and faux piercings. If a scene in your movie calls for a sweaty athlete, douse the actor with baby oil. Or if you need to age a character well past her 16 years, massage flour in her hair and she'll be a white-haired old lady in no time.

Need a beard for a boy who hasn't hit puberty? Just a little cold cream and coffee grounds applied to his face should do the trick. A painful bruise? Draw one on your actor with nontoxic, washable magic markers—use red, then cover it with blue and smear the two together on their skin. Ouch, that looks like it hurts!

To create a disgustingly real cut on someone's body, use fake blood and black eyeliner to make the slash. If it makes you say, "Yuck," you know you've got it right. Finally, for sci-fi fans, you can simulate a mean radiation burn (guaranteed to make your audience squirm) by mixing unflavored gelatin (yes, that's Jell-O without the taste) with food coloring to make it red. Or you can mix Vaseline and fake blood for the same purpose. Apply either substance to your actor's skin. The gelatin mixture dries quickly, so work fast if you use it.

And whatever you do, don't forget the bulging eye which can be easily crafted with half a ping pong ball. Scary!

"One of the greatest things about making a film is that they have a life of their own outside the box office. I recently heard that a women's group in Sri Lanka screened 'Bhaji on the Beach'—I hear from women across the world who have watched my films—women, especially women of color—are starved for stories. Your audience is the world!"

GURINDER CHADHA

Be smart—if you're going to use fake blood on your set, make sure everyone around knows it's only Karo syrup. Don't want to freak out innocent bystanders, do we?

While we're on the subject of bruises,

every once in a while you may want to make a movie that calls for a little fake gore, right? Maybe a bit of blood, or a couple of nasty looking lacerations or radiation burns? For fake blood, ketchup always works wonders, but our good friends at *Exposure* (*www.exposure.co.uk*) recommend this more sophisticated recipe:

- 16 oz. Karo syrup (it's in the grocery store)
- 1 oz. red food coloring
- 1 oz. washing detergent or dish soap
- 1 oz. water

Mix together and add maybe a drop of blue food coloring for a more realistic look. Don't eat it (gross!) and be careful because the blood substance is extremely sticky, stains clothing, and sometimes your skin. Wash off quickly.

"Someday I hope to work with a budget that allows me to shoot action—shooting with cranes or helicopters, explosions, and fight scenes. So far in my career, I've done action shots and stunts on a very low budget.

"For instance, when we were shooting 'Godass,' we had to shoot a car crash but couldn't afford a stunt car, or, for that matter, stunt actors. So we just found a deserted street and went for it. When my lead actor, Nika Feldman, wasn't throwing herself into the windshield on her mark, I had to show her how. It hurt. But I thought it was great fun. You've got to be game for trying anything for the sake of the film."

ESTHER BELL

Esther Bell

Esther on the set of her first feature film, Godass. *She paid her way through college by working on film productions and now she's got her own production company,* Hells Bells. *Her films include an award-winning documentary* Mark of an Amateur, *and many short films including* Happy Daze, Vampire in Slo Mo, *and* Get up! Get out! *Check out her Web site www.estherbell.com.*

Sometimes a sound can substitute for something you can't show visually—like explosions or animal noises (anyone got an extra llama around?). Have someone off camera make the sound as your characters react as if it occurred out of frame.

Snazzy Sound Effects

If you record your movie with a camcorder or DV camera, always remember that visuals are only half of what your camera is picking up—it's also recording *sound*. You can create a whole host of special sound effects right in your backyard or bedroom. People who create specialized *sound effects* for movies are called *Foley Artists* and, to them, making noise is an art form. They use simple, everyday objects to create a symphony of cool sounds.

Designate a pal to be the Foley Artist on your set, and give her a few ideas to begin with. Soon she'll get in the groove and create some original noises just for your movie. You can make them while you shoot or record them separately as audio components of your movie. Here are a few examples of common background sounds:

Snow

Sprinkle cornstarch on the floor and ask someone to walk across it. Sounds like snow!

Rain

Drop grains of rice or birdseed onto a cookie sheet (for a rooftop effect) or a plastic container (sounds like a shower outside). Or, if you're recording near the bathroom, just turn on the shower!

Thunder

Take a piece of sheet metal and shake it, occasionally striking the sheet's surface with the palm of your hand to add rumbles. Add some falling rice to the mix and it's a full-blown downpour.

Footsteps

Depending on the surface your character is walking across, you can use a variety of objects to simulate the sound of her shoes hitting the

floor. Wooden blocks struck slowly together usually work. But say you're character's wearing heels on a linoleum floor—bang a couple of CD cases together, and *click, click, click*—she's walking across the floor.

Car Crashes

Place a few small trinkets of glass, metal, coins, or keys into a paper milk carton. Then shake the carton while you hit it with your hand just once. Add to the effect by dropping a few pieces of glass against a hard surface. (BE CAREFUL PLEASE.) Eerie silence should follow.

Animals

Meow, bark, or moo. You'll want to get the right pitch so listen to your pets.

Fights

You may need a few POWs or PUNCHes for your Kung Fu flick—so take a ruler and slap it flatly on the cushions of a sofa or plush chair. Ouch! For broken bones, snap a twig in two near your camera's microphone. A few good screams from your actor/victim will complete this effect.

Explosions

Depending upon the type of explosion you want, the sound can range from popping a balloon to a big fireworks bang. Just making a loud noise sometimes does the trick.

All sorts of other sound effects are easy to make if you use your imagination and pay attention to the noises you hear everyday. Also, sound effects recordings are readily available on the Internet, so log on for a listen and then figure out what you can use to make a similar sound. Experiment!

More On-Screen Shenanigans

Climb the Walls

By setting your camera or camcorder on its side you can defy gravity. First, find a location without a lot of objects in the background. Set the camera up on its side and ask a cast member to act as if they are scaling a wall, or climbing up a steep mountain. With the right framing, no viewer will ever know that huge mountain is really your flat backyard. Or that Batgirl isn't scaling a building, but actually crawling on her hands and knees on a brick sidewalk.

Split Screen

You know that funny technique you always see on sitcoms—when Ethel and Lucy (or Buffy and Willow) call each other on the phone? Sure you do, the screen *splits* into two sections so you can see them at the same time talking on the phone. Well, that's a split screen.

You can create a similar illusion by placing two sets directly next to each other. Frame your shot to include the two sets. Each should have different wallpaper, drapes or posters, and other contrasts like dissimilar props, lighting, and furniture. Then frame your shot to include both sets. Record your actors alternately speaking into their phones. (They are having a conversation after all.) If you do this trick right, it will look like they're miles apart.

FUN FILTERS

Filters are glass or gelatin materials that fit over your camera's lens to alter light as it passes through the camera. They can add contrast to an image or soften it. They can also reduce glare or add other effects, like fog. For the most part, filters are the domain of professional cinematographers, because knowing *how* and *when* to use them requires know-how and additional equipment. But using a filter doesn't have to be complicated—if you're creative, you can engineer your own low-tech approach.

Make a colored filter by placing a lightweight, see-through piece of fabric in front of your lens. For a far-out look, stick a sheet of magnifying paper (or Grandma's bifocals) in front of the lens—how's that look? Anything you put in front of the lens (that light can pass through) is a *filter*—so feel free to play around and see what else you can use.

If you buy a protective clear filter you can apply other filters directly to the camera. A little Vaseline, for instance, smeared across the protective lens makes a really cool blurry effect.

MAKE A MATTE

Mattes, or matte boards, are like filters in that they go in front of the camera's lens to create a special effect. All it takes to make a matte is a piece of cardboard or some heavy black construction paper. Simply cut out a shape in the paper as a frame through which you'll record or film. Used this way, a matte is just a picture frame attached to the front of your camera.

Some obvious examples: cut 2 attached circles out of the middle of the cardboard, and hold it directly in front of the lens. Look through your viewfinder and it'll seem like you're looking through binoculars. You can use the same technique to create other matte effects—windows, keyholes, peepholes—you get the idea.

Another fun way to use mattes is to make cardboard cut-outs to place in front of the camera. Make a cut-out in the shape of a monster, paint it black and it looks like a silhouette through the lens. Then record your actors' reactions to the monster. Saves you some time finding that perfect *Creature from the Deep* costume, now doesn't it?

Forced Perspective

By positioning one friend (say, *Harper*) close to the camera and another (say, *Drew*) far behind her, you can create the illusion that Harper's holding Drew in the palm of her hand. Here's how:

Ask Harper to stand slightly to the side in your frame and to stretch out her hand as if she's holding up something. Then position Drew (who's a good distance away) so that it looks like he's standing right in Harper's hand. Funny!

Don't stop with people. Harper's so tough, she can pick up anything—cows, trees, and trucks. Now you've got your very own SuperGirl.

Camera-Less Movies?

Make a Movie without a Camera

Are you serious? Yes, it's true, you can make a movie without a camera or a computer. So you gals who couldn't find a camera *anywhere*—don't fret. And even if you do have a camera, these techniques create such great effects that you should try them anyway.

Draw on Film

What you need:

- ✎ Clear Super 8 film leader, or clear 16mm film leader (it's a bigger size film format). You can buy either one at any specialty camera or photography store. (Or check out the Kodak Web site.)
- ✎ Thin-tipped markers. (Just the ones specifically for film—buy them at an art store. I've gotten a bunch of different colors for about $1 a piece.)

Clear leader is the stuff that's used to help thread a projector before an actual film runs. But you can make an entire animated movie out of it by drawing pictures or images directly onto it—no camera needed.

First, tape down some blank, white paper on your workspace. Then roll off about a foot of clear leader to use later when you thread your projector. With the rest of the film spool in your lap, spool off the leader vertically in front of you. Then using markers, draw on the emulsion side of the film (that's the dull looking side).

You can draw any image you like—abstract shapes, words, sketches of people—anything. Just keep it simple, because you'll need to draw *a lot* of images and in a really tiny space. Remember that for every 18 images you draw, you'll only get one second of screen time. So it's important to make the figures you draw very basic. And use fine-point pens!

When you finish creating your drawings, rewind the film onto the reel and project it with a Super 8 film projector. See—there's your animated movie, and you did it without even picking up a camera! Pretty amazing, huh?

Drawing on film is a great group project since you need so many different drawings to make a short movie. Find a long table, or spread blank pieces of paper on the floor to place your clear leader on, and provide a selection of pens. Collaborate with a few pals—each of you can work on separate sections of film at the same time. You'll finish your animated film in half the time!

"I keep making films from a continued desire to show people what is usually not shown, to speak what is usually not spoken, and to create complex characters. As a filmmaker, you've got to look beneath the surface of things and tell stories about what's there. So look at the world around you—live life and take chances. Then you have something to make movies about!"

BETTE GORDON

Bette Gordon

Bette is an independent filmmaker who is known for her bold explorations of themes related to sexuality and identity. Her films include Empty Suitcases, Variety, *and* Luminous Motion.

Expert Advice from Su Friedrich

Scratching on Film

"Another way to draw on film is to actually scratch on the emulsion side of the film, which you can do on black leader or any film that has an image. If you do it on color film, you'll see bits of each of the three layers of dye (red, green, and blue) that are in the emulsion, which can look really cool. Color film is a lot softer, so it's easy to scratch on. Black leader, or black & white film, is harder because of the silver in the emulsion, so it helps to moisten the film slightly by wiping it with a wet finger (but a clean finger, or you leave bits of dirt on the film!). The best tool to use is an engraver's tool—a pen-like instrument with exchangeable steel tips. If you can't find one, you can use a push pin or a straight pin, but it makes for sore fingers after a while! You can tape a straight pin to a pencil to make it easier to hold. The other tricky thing is that, if you're working with original, you have to write backwards because otherwise, when you project it, the words will be flipped. A little practice makes perfect."

After you've finished scratching your film to reveal the image you want, take a piece of velvet or soft cotton fabric and wipe off the scraps of loose film emulsion. Then, if you wish, you can also color in the clear area with a permanent marker.

Warning: These two techniques—drawing and scratching on film, can only be done on FILM. Videotape cannot be scratched on!

Su often uses this technique in her films. A frame from her film Gently Down the Stream *shows text scratched beside images.*

Interactive Movies

What could possibly be more fun for your audience than to be part of the movie? Make an interactive movie by planning ahead—record your actor having one side of a conversation. Then, when you screen your flick, plant an audience member to pretend to have a conversation with the actor up on screen.

The trickiest part of drawing on film is making sure your drawing falls within the frame of the film. Since Super 8 film leader doesn't have any frame lines (it's blank) you'll have to figure out ahead of time the area of film to draw on. Do this by locating the perforations on the side of the strip of leader. These perforations fall roughly in the center of each individual frame—so you can center your drawing on the strip by lining it up with the perforation. That way you can be sure the image you draw will appear the same on screen.

Chapter Eleven

Digital Dames Direct

Stuff You'll Need

If you want to make a movie on a computer from scratch, you'll need more than just editing software. Consider adding:

- **drawing and illustrating programs,**
- **graphic design programs,**
- **multimedia programs, and/or**
- **a scanner.**

Okay—You wired wonderchicks have been flipping through this book, with one hand on a keyboard, wondering why I haven't mentioned the D-Word sooner. *I know what you're thinking: This girl is whack with all this Super 8 and video stuff—I know I can make a movie right here on my desktop computer.* Well, um, you're right. You can make a movie from start to finish using just a personal computer. Your trusty PC or Mac (and the right software) can do it all: edit your footage, enhance your footage, even *build* the footage (by scanning pictures, photographs, or drawing on your desktop).

There are lots of moviemaking programs out there for people like us: beginning moviemakers who know their way around a Web page, but who don't have much cashola. Editing systems and multimedia programs that only the pros used to have are now available to the general consumer. See, a big Hollywood moviemaker might pay $500 a day for the use of a computer-based editing system. You, on the other hand, can purchase a similar sort of software, install it on your computer and it's yours for life, not just one day.

But it's still not cheap—probably a few hundred bucks, which I'm guessing you *don't* have lying around your room. A couple of these programs may be available through your school computer lab or community center. (They may have even come bundled on your home computer.)

All right, so you are a digital diva and you want to know how to use your computer savvy to make (or finish) a dazzling movie. There are countless ways to go, so I'll just outline a few . . .

NOVICES IN A NON-LINEAR WORLD

If you've shot your footage on a video or DV camcorder (for Super 8 you'll need a video transfer), and want to edit the movie using a computer, follow these steps:

1. Digitize your footage.

To do this you'll need a gizmo called a *capture card* for your computer. The other choice is a *FireWire* connection, which allows you to hook your camcorder directly to your computer. Most of today's computers have one of these components already. If not, save those pennies—it's upgrade time.

Digitizing transforms your video footage into digital files on your computer's hard drive. If you have a lot of footage, you may have too little memory to digitize the whole movie at one time. Work in short sections, and then digitize more footage as you free space on the hard drive. (You'll free up this space as you select the footage you want and delete the files you don't.)

2. Set up that software.

After your raw footage is digitized, you're ready to go. (Provided you've gotten your hands on an editing program.) If you haven't, start looking, or plan a fund-raiser—even low-grade editing software is pretty costly.

Once you're set up, welcome to the non-linear world! Now, you can access any part of your footage with a click of the mouse. This makes selecting and compiling shots really easy. What's non-linear? It's like finding your favorite song on a CD (track four) at the touch of a button, rather than fast-forwarding through a cassette tape.

3. Save that file!

When you finish editing your flick, save your movie as a computer file, or export it back to your camera. Watch it on the computer monitor or on the TV screen.

Don't have a computer? Go to your local library—they do!

So why did I hold out on giving you the computer moviemaking skinny?

A couple of reasons.

First of all, there are so many different multimedia software programs on the market today that it would take an encyclopedia to describe all of them, and then an entire book on how to use them. Here are a few of the lead programs at the time of this writing: Premiere, Director, Final-Cut Pro, Flash, After Effects, and iMovie. And as we all know, these programs will probably be replaced, updated, or joined by many more—probably in the next year.

The second reason has more to do with training; namely, before you ride a motorcycle, you should learn to ride a bike. Get what I mean? Before you become a whiz at using a moviemaking computer set-up, it helps to understand the fundamentals of filmmaking. And you can learn those using a pen and paper and flipbook. In other words, get your basic toolbox stocked up—then you can move on to the fancy stuff.

> "You live now in a world of DV and desktop editing—GO MAKE FILMS. The first one will suck, so make another one after that."
>
> BRONWEN HUGHES

Worldwide Audience

Whether or not you *make* your movie on a computer, you will probably want it to be *seen* on one. Thousands, millions of them, if possible. If you haven't guessed, this section is about getting your movie online. The fact is, the Internet is the friendliest place around for short movies. It's a great venue for getting your movie seen—24-hours-a-day by a worldwide audience. And the Internet is perfect for super short movies, since they compress easily into small files and don't require lots of time to download. There are tons of online film festivals and Web cinemas looking for beginners just like you—short moviemakers who won't charge them an arm and a leg for new and exciting content. Of course, they won't show your movie forever, so build your own Web site and include clips, or a full-on screening for other Web travelers and short movie lovers.

To get your flick ready to go online, you'll need to digitize it and compress it to a file format designed for Internet delivery (QuickTime, RealVideo, or MPEG-1). Then find a webserver, or online festival that will host your flick. (Better yet build the site yourself.) Make your movie's presence known on the Web by promoting your site through mass e-mail.

Some tips for internet flicks:

1. **Make it short.** Short, short movies work best on the Internet. People surf so quickly around the Web that they aren't likely to sit and watch a 30-minute movie, even if it is brilliant.
2. **Engage the audience instantly.** Again, there's so much out there on the Web that you've got to snag your audience fast. Your short has to look more interesting than that banner ad for free MP3 downloads.
3. **Get lots of close-ups.** Since the screen size is usually quite small for online flicks, keep your shots tight and actions relatively sparse. That way the movie will screen well on computer monitors.
4. **Keep the file size down.** No one likes to wait for a long download. Your audience will lose interest quickly if you make them wait all day for your movie to download.
5. **Give 'em something to look at during downloads.** Add more info about the movie to the page, if possible. Also include your e-mail address so fans can contact you—that's the best part!

Now get started— the world is waiting.

GIRL DIRECTORS, TAKE OVER THE WORLD!

ESSENTIAL ZINES

FEMME FLICKE
Super-smart articles and commentary on lady-made movies and the women who make 'em. Write editor Tina Spangler by snail mail for your copy: Femme Flicke, 246 Seventh Ave. #10, Brooklyn, NY 11215.

Illustration: Lucie Chan

FILM AND DESTROY
This e-zine sports great graphics and is a cornucopia of resources and motivation for the girl moviemaker. Check out the latest at *www.sirius.com/~otterfd/filmdesl.htm.*

FLICKER: YOUR GUIDE TO THE WORLD OF SUPER 8

If you're going to shoot Super 8, keep this handy guide in your back pocket at all times! Also, look for info on the Flicker Film Festival, which might just be coming through your town. *www.flickerla.com*

FESTIVALS

BACKYARD NATIONAL CHILDREN'S FILM FESTIVAL
This is the only international festival that celebrates movies made by kids ages 18 and under. The festival includes discussions with industry pros and workshops for young moviemakers. Networked with science museums and youth museums throughout the U.S. and Canada, there might be a local chapter that hosts workshops and festivities in your city.
www.childrensfilmfest.org
www.backyardfilm.org

CINEMAKIDS
A non-competitive program that screens films and videos created by youth. This cool new program is a part of the pioneering short film festival, Cinematexas in Austin, TX. *www.uts.cc.utexas.edu/~cinematx/cinemakids.html*

DIF/FUSION
Now in its 8th year, Dif/fusion screens and celebrates independent film and video made by women of color. The festival happens in Santa Cruz, CA, but accepts submissions from gals of color anywhere. *www2.ucsc.edu/people/andysm/filmfest/index.htm*

GOLDEN TRAILER AWARDS
Filmmaker and Girl Director advisee Esther Bell clued me in on this project. Cut your film into a trailer or just make a trailer and submit it to the no-budget category. *www.goldentrailer.com*

HERE'S LOOKING AT YOU KID
A festival for, by, and about girls sponsored by the Lower Eastside Girls Club in New York City. Filmmaker Jan Albert directs this annual festival that takes place in October.

LADYFEST
A non-profit, community-based event designed by and for women that happens every year in various locales. Six blissful days of all-girl activities including bands, workshops, speakers, and most importantly—film & video screenings. *www.ladyfest.org.*

MADCAT: WOMEN'S INTERNATIONAL FILM FESTIVAL

International film festival held annually in San Francisco, but that also hits the road as a touring show. E-mail Director Ariella Ben-Dov, and say either "here's my movie" or "come to my town too."
www.somaglow.com/madcat.

FILM & VIDEO ORGANIZATIONS

GRIT—GIRLS REELING IT TOGETHER
This group of writer/directors' mission is to highlight the work of women filmmakers and cultivate an audience for these great films—a sort of "Lilith Fair of Short Film." Write *girlsreelingittogether@yahoo.com* for more info on what you can do to get gritty.

MR LADY RECORDS & VIDEOS
Distributor of affordable movies by independent video artists and filmmakers. Great stuff! *www.mrlady.com*

THIRD WORLD NEWSREEL
Started in 1967 as a network of radical filmmakers this organization is committed to developing artists and audiences of color. Today they distribute the work of over 200 media artists and offer workshops, production, and technical support for moviemakers. *www.twn.org*

WOMEN IN THE DIRECTOR'S CHAIR
A Chicago-based media arts center that exhibits, promotes, and educates about media made by women that expresses a diversity of cultures, experiences and issues. WIDC sponsors an annual touring festival of films and videos by women and girls. *www.widc.org*

WOMEN MAKE MOVIES
The largest distributor of media made by women in the nation. In addition to that, they also put on seminars, hold screenings, and offer a fiscal sponsorship program. *www.wmm.com*

MEDIA ACCESS CENTERS

These are the kind folks you go to for advice on how to find equipment, facilities, and educational programs. There are hundreds of these hip joints across the U.S., so don't lose hope if it's not listed here.

FILM ARTS FOUNDATION
For 25 years FAF has provided affordable services and equipment to San Francisco moviemakers. And the AEIOU (Alternative Exhibition Information of the Universe) guide is a must if you're taking your show on the road. *www.filmarts.org*

MIDWEST MEDIA ARTISTS ACCESS CENTER
Offers low-cost access to all sorts of equipment and facilities in a supportive and educational environment. They also have a women filmmakers grant and lots of beginner classes. *www.mtn.org/mmaac*

NATIONAL ALLIANCE FOR MEDIA ARTS AND CULTURE
An amazing organization, and their site contains links to alternative media sites nationwide. *www.namac.org*

REEL WOMEN
Based in Austin, Texas this nonprofit organization is a wonderful support system for women at all levels of experience in moviemaking. *www.reelwomen.org*

SQUEAKY WHEEL/ BUFFALO MEDIA RESOURCES
Supports and promotes film, video, and digital art by independent and community moviemakers in Buffalo, NY. *www.squeaky.org*

STREET- LEVEL YOUTH MEDIA
Using video production, computer art, and the Internet, Street-Level Youth Media educates and provides equipment for inner-city Chicago youth. So cool! *www.streetlevel.iit.edu*

MOVIE PLACES NOT TO MISS

AMERICAN MUSEUM OF THE MOVING IMAGE
The most fun you'll ever have in a museum, I promise. Located in Queens, NY. *www.ammi.org*

ANTHOLOGY FILM ARCHIVES
Preserves and exhibits all sorts of classic and contemporary independent and avant-garde film and video. Located in NYC. *www.anthologyfilmarchives.org*

PROCESSING PLACES

(You only need these if you're shooting Super 8!)

Check your town, there might be a local place that processes Super 8 film. If not, here are a few favorites:

YALE FILM AND VIDEO
Located in North Hollywood, CA, these folks can set any Super 8 moviemaker up—processing, rentals, and even film-to-video transfers are all available. Send them your film from anywhere. *www.yalefilmandvideo.com*

DWAYNE'S PHOTO
Dwayne's has been processing film since 1956. Current clients include NBC, HBO, and the NBA—and now they can add your Super 8 film to the mix. *www.k-14movies.com*

GIRL DIRECTOR BIBLIOGRAPHY

The Animation Book
Kit Laybourne
Crown Publishing Group, 1998

Birth of the Motion Picture
Emmanuelle Toulet
Harry N. Abrams, Inc., 1995

Calling the Shots: Profiles of Women Filmmakers
Janis Cole and Holly Dale
Quarry Press, 1994

Camcorder Tricks and Special Effects
Michael Stavros
Amherst Media, Inc., 1999

Chick Flicks: Theories and Memories of the Feminist Film Movement
B. Ruby Rich
Duke University Press, 1998

Cinematography
Kris Malkiewicz
Simon and Schuster, 1992

The Complete Kodak Animation Book
Charles Solomon
Eastman Kodak Company, 1983

Dictionary of Film Terms: The Aesthetic Companion to Film Analysis
Frank Beaver
McMillian Library Reference,1994

Directed by Dorothy Arzner
Judith Mayne
Indiana University Press, 1994

Film Fatales: Independent Women Directors
Judith M. Redding and Victoria A. Brownworth
Seal Press, 1997

Film Lighting
Kris Malkiewicz
Simon and Schuster, 1986

Frame by Frame: A Handbook for Creative Filmmaking
Eric Sherman
Acrobat Books, 1987

Getting Into Film
Mel London
Ballantine Books, 1985

Make Your Own Animated Movies and Videotapes
Yvonne Andersen
Little, Brown, and Company, 1991

Reel Women: Pioneers of the Cinema 1896 to the Present
Ally Acker
The Continuum Publishing Company, 1991

Setting Up Your Shots: Great Camera Moves Every Fillmmaker Should Know
Jeremy Vineyard
Michaael Wiese Productions, 1999

The Silent Feminists: America's First Women Directors
Anthony Slide
A.S. Barnes and Company, Inc., 1996

The St. James Women Filmmakers Encyclopedia: Women on the Other Side of the Camera
Edited by Amy L. Unterburger
Visible Ink Press, 1999

When Women Call the Shots: The Developing Power and Influence of Women in Television and Film
Linda Seger
Henry Holt and Company, 1996

Without Lying Down: Frances Marion and the Powerful Women of Early Hollywood
Cari Beauchamp
University of California Press, 1998

The Women's Companion to International Film
Edited by Annette Kuhn with Susannah Radstone
University of California Press, 1994

You Stand There: Making Music Video
David Kleiler and Robert Moses
Three Rivers Press, 1997

PHOTO CREDITS

Cover
Agnès Varda, courtesy of Agnès Varda, Ciné-Tamaris, and the Academy of Motion Picture Arts and Sciences. Photo © Ciné-Tamaris.

Back Cover
Ida Lupino, courtesy of the Academy of Motion Picture Arts and Sciences; Lina Wertmuller, courtesy of the Academy of Motion Picture Arts and Sciences and Lina Wertmuller; Leslie Harris, courtesy of Leslie Harris, photo by Mel Wright; Amy Heckerling, courtesy of Columbia/Tristar Pictures and Amy Heckerling, photo by Mary E. Matthews from *Loser,* © 2000 Columbia Pictures.

p. iv-v Mabel Normand, courtesy of the Museum of Modern Art film stills archive.
p. vii Allison Anders, courtesy of Bumble Ward and Allison Anders.

Intro
p. 3 Photo of Amy Heckerling by Mary E. Matthews, from *Loser*, © 2000 Columbia Pictures Industries, Inc. All rights reserved. Courtesy of Columbia/Tristar Pictures and Amy Heckerling.

Chapter 1
p. 4 Alice Guy Blaché, courtesy of the Academy of Motion Picture Arts and Sciences.
p. 5 Alice Guy Blaché, courtesy of the Academy of Motion Picture Arts and Sciences.
p. 6 Alice Guy Blaché, courtesy of the Academy of Motion Picture Arts and Sciences.
p. 8 Lois Weber, courtesy of the Women Film Pioneers Project and Marc Wannamaker at Bison Films Stills Archive.
p. 11 Mabel Normand, courtesy of the Academy of Motion Picture Arts and Sciences.
p. 12 Frances Marion and Mary Pickford, courtesy of The Academy of Motion Picture Arts and Sciences.
p. 13 Mary Pickford, courtesy of Marc Wanamaker at Bison Films Stills Archive.
p. 13 Mary Pickford and Douglas Fairbanks, courtesy of The Academy of Motion Picture Arts and Sciences.
p. 14 Lillian and Dorothy Gish, courtesy of the Academy of Motion Picture Arts and Sciences.
p. 16 Maya Deren, courtesy of Anthology Film Archives.
p. 17 Dorothy Arzner, courtesy of the Academy of Motion Picture Arts and Sciences.
p. 18 Ida Lupino, courtesy of the Academy of Motion Picture Arts and Sciences.
p. 19 Ida Lupino, courtesy of the Academy of Motion Picture Arts and Sciences.

Chapter 2
p. 21 Kate Haug, courtesty of Kate Haug.
p. 21 Britta Sjogren, courtesy of Britta Sjogren.
p. 22 Laura Nix, courtesy of Laura Nix.
p. 26 Barbara Kopple, courtesy of Cabin Creek Films and Barbara Kopple.
p. 29 Penelope Spheeris, courtesy of Penelope Spheeris.
p. 31 Nancy Savoca, courtesy of Nancy Savoca.
p. 31 Leslie Harris on the set of *Bessie Coleman: A Dream to Fly*, Showtime Network, courtesy of Leslie Harris. Photo by Mel Wright.
p. 31 Joan Chen, courtesy of Joan Chen.

Chapter 3
p. 32 Naomi Uman, courtesy of Naomi Uman.
p. 37 Bronwen Hughes, courtesy of Bronwen Hughes. Photo by Lindsay Skutch.
p. 38 Melinda Stone, courtesy of Melinda Stone.
p. 39 Katherine Dieckmann, courtesy of Katherine Dieckmann.

Chapter 4
p. 46 Deepa Mehta, from *Camilla*, 1993, photo by Dilip Mehta, courtesy of Deepa Mehta.
p. 49 Photo of Sarah Jacobson by Lee Jacobson, courtesy of Sarah Jacobson.
p. 49 Tamra Davis, courtesy of Trimark Pictures and Tamra Davis, photo by Chris Helgermanas-Benge.

Chapter 5
p. 53 Stacy Cochran, courtesy of Stacy Cochran and Spencer Newman. © Drop Back Ten, Inc. 2000.
p. 54 Mary Ann Henry, courtesy of Mary Ann Henry.
p. 56 Margie Schnibbe, courtesy of Margie Schnibbe.
p. 60 Catherine Hollander, courtesy of Catherine Hollander.
p. 61 Nora Ephron, courtesy of Nora Ephron.
p. 61 Jane Anderson, courtesy of Jane Anderson.

Chapter 6
p. 62 Gillian Armstrong, courtesy of Gillian Armstrong and Hilary Linstead Associates.
p. 64 Su Friedrich, courtesy of Su Friedrich.
p. 65 Jocelyn Moorhouse, courtesy ofJocelyn Moorhouse.
p. 69 Susan Seidelman, courtesty of Susan Seidelman.
p. 70 Melanie Mayron, courtesy of Melanie Mayron.
p. 73 Gurinder Chadha, courtesy of Trimark Pictures and Gurinder Chadha.
p. 74 Melanie Mayron, courtesy of Melanie Mayron.

Chapter 7
p. 76 Martha Coolidge, courtesy of Martha Coolidge.
p. 77 Lizzie Borden, courtesy of First Run Features and Lizzie Borden.
p. 78 Rita Gonzalez, courtesy of Rita Gonzalez.
p. 80 Lina Wertmuller, courtesy of the Academy of Motion Picture Arts and Sciences and Lina Wertmuller.
p. 83 Bronwen Hughes, courtesy of Bronwen Hughes.
p. 84 Women at Biograph Studios, courtesy of the Museum of Modern Art film stills archive.
p. 84 Verna Fields, courtesy of The Academy of Motion Picture Arts and Sciences.
p. 86 Barbara Kopple, courtesy of Cabin Creek Films and Barbara Kopple.
p. 86 Agnès Varda, courtesy of Agnès Varda, Ciné-Tamaris, and the Academy of Motion Picture Arts and Sciences. Photo © Ciné-Tamaris.
p. 87 Lina Wertmuller, courtesy of Lina Wertmuller and Carol Levi & Company.

Chapter 8
p. 88 Irene Turner, photo by Peggy Pierce, courtesy of Irene Turner.
p. 89 Tamra Davis, courtesy of Trimark Pictures and Tamra Davis.
p. 90 Karyn Kusama, photo by Theresa Dillon, courtesy of MPRM and Karyn Kusama.
p. 94 Melinda Stone, Kate Haug, and Vera Edelson, photo by Igor Vamos, courtesy of Melinda Stone.
p. 95 Miranda July, courtesy of Miranda July.

Chapter 9
p. 99 Tina Bastajian, courtesy of Tina Bastajian. Photo by Melissa Levin.
p. 102 Maggie Greenwald, courtesy of Trimark Pictures and Maggie Greenwald.
p. 106 Mary Ellen Bute, courtesy of Anthology Film Archives. Photo by Ted Nemeth.
p. 106 Martha Colburn, courtesy of Martha Colburn.

Chapter 10
p. 108 Mary Pickford, courtesy of the Academy of Motion Picture Arts and Sciences.
p. 109 Cheryl Dunye, photo by Dan Dennehy for Walker Arts Center, courtesy of First Run Features and Cheryl Dunye.
p. 110 Allison Anders, courtesy of Allison Anders.
p. 114 Esther Bell with Milton Kam (DP) and Rachel Levine (AD), courtesy of Esther Bell. Photo by Sarah Vanburen.
p. 117 Bette Gordon, courtesy of Bette Gordon.
p. 117 Still from *Gently Down the Stream,* courtesy of Su Friedrich.

p. 122 Dorothy Gish, courtesy of the Academy of Motion Picture Arts and Sciences.

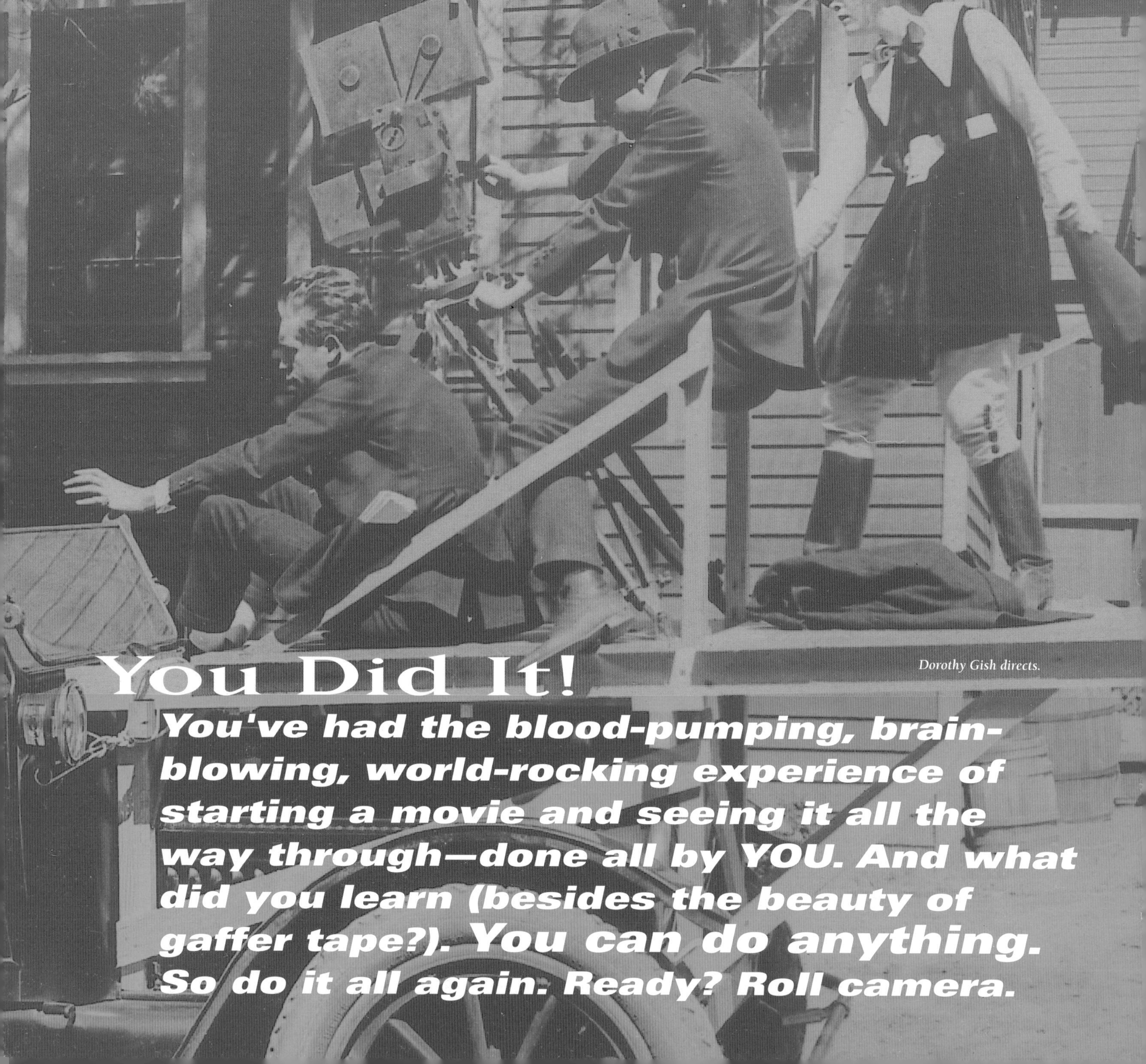

Dorothy Gish directs.

You Did It!

You've had the blood-pumping, brain-blowing, world-rocking experience of starting a movie and seeing it all the way through—done all by YOU. And what did you learn (besides the beauty of gaffer tape?). You can do anything. So do it all again. Ready? Roll camera.